What Others Are Sa
Loving Your Wife as Christ Loves the Church

Loving Your Wife as Christ Loves the Church is convicting, challenging, and instructive. It is convicting because it exposes ways in which most of us are not loving our wives, challenging because it sets before us the biblical standard for husbands, and instructive because Pastor McCall shows us how to mend our ways and where we get the power to do it. Since we all are still "in process," every husband, regardless of how long he's been married, will profit from this book.

> **Jerry Bridges**, conference speaker and author of
> several books, including *The Pursuit of Holiness,*
> and *The Discipline of Grace*

The command that a man should love his wife "as Christ loves the church" is a jewel of truth shining like a diamond in Ephesians 5. McCall lifts this diamond out of the text and through clear, thorough exposition exposes the many facets of what it means to love like Christ. *Loving Your Wife as Christ Loves the Church* is a pleasure to read. McCall's love for Christ and for his wife is on every page.

> **Dr. Tedd Tripp**, Pastor, Conference Speaker,
> Author of *Shepherding a Child's Heart*

In our work with men over the past eight years I have been on a quest to find a book for men that focuses on the gospel of Jesus Christ as it applies to helping men know how to love their wives, as the need in this area is so great. My quest is over. *Loving Your Wife as Christ Loves the Church*, by Dr. Larry McCall is a masterful work that will no doubt have a great impact on men of all walks of life who desire to learn how to truly love their wives. We are encouraging all the men in our ministry to read this book because we believe it will change hearts, marriages, and lives everywhere.

> **Mike Cleveland**, Pastor of Preaching and Vision,
> Ohio Valley Church, Medina, Ohio;
> Founder and President of Setting Captives Free Ministries

With razor-sharp clarity, Pastor Larry McCall puts "feet" on what it means to love one's wife as Christ loves the church. This book is a must-read for any husband no longer satisfied with a mediocre marriage relationship. I am both convicted and challenged to love my wife better. *Loving Your Wife As Christ Loves the Church* is my gift to all our pastors.

> **Hutz H. Hertzberg**, D. Min., Ph.D., Executive Pastor, The Moody Church, Chicago, Illinois

Larry McCall applies 30 years of pastoral experience, biblical studies, and lessons from his own marriage to guide you through the turbulent, uncharted waters of marriage. This practical, easy-to-read book will offer hope, comfort, and encouragement.

> **Todd Wilson**, Familyman Ministries

Larry McCall has given us husbands a gospel-centered, grace-filled and practical book. Larry holds before our eyes the love of Christ for His church, like a gem of many beautiful facets, and invites us to explore and apply the truth of each facet to our marriages. This book has challenged and inspired me to pursue Christ and imitate His love in my own marriage.

> **Mark Altrogge**, Senior Pastor of Sovereign Grace Church of Indiana, Pennsylvania, and writer of worship music

This is wonderful book, not only for husbands in troubled marriages, but also for any husband who has a desire to grow in his understanding and practice of Christ-like love for his wife. Masculine culture falsely assumes such love comes naturally. On the contrary, Dr. McCall clearly demonstrates that it requires careful attention to the selfless love of Christ. A woman's heart will naturally want to respond to that type of love.

> **Dr. John D. Street**, Chair, MABC graduate program, The Master's College & Seminary, Santa Clarita, California

I enthusiastically welcome Dr. Larry McCall's book! To heed Jesus' command to love our wife as He loves His church requires an understanding that the author is very clearly defining and expounding, not only for married men, but also for those who are preparing to become husbands. I fully believe that it is only the kind of relationship between husband and wife taught in Ephesians 5:22-23 which will honor the Lord Jesus Christ, which will offer a credible testimony and practical example of the relationship between Christ and His bride, and which will provide a very indispensable foundation in Christ's service.

Joe Aleppo, President/Executive Director,
Aurora Ministries and Mission, Bradenton, Florida

Through a careful study of the nature of Christ's love for the church, Larry McCall provides timely guidance for current and future husbands that is unapologetically biblical and profoundly practical. Readers will not only find themselves praising the Lord anew for His incomparable love for the church, but will also now recognize that the Lord Jesus' call to follow in His steps applies even to our marriages.

Martin M. Culy, Associate Professor of New Testament
and Greek, Briercrest College and Seminary,
Caronport, SK, CANADA

Author and Pastor Larry McCall brings experience into his writing and raises the biblical standard for men. Loving your wife as Christ loved the church is a calling that demands some refresher courses. Here's one that will do you good!

Jim Elliff, President, Christian Communicators Worldwide,
Parkville, Missouri

Larry McCall displays the rare combination of a sound theology and a pastor's heart. In his book, husbands will discover not only God's precepts for marriage, but also very practical ways to implement them. Pastor McCall puts the emphasis where it belongs—on the choice of the husband rather than the response of his wife.

Tom Edgington, Professor of Counseling, Grace College
and Grace Theological Seminary, Winona Lake, Indiana.

This is a needed book. Multitudes of Christian books have been written about every aspect of marriage, but Larry McCall's book zooms in on the distinct privilege of loving your wife, as a joint heir of grace—yes, that means, loving a sinner like you! It's to be expected, considering who we men are. Too many Christian men enter into the husband role assuming a posture of near-omnipotence. Larry's book humbles us back into our rightful posture as fellow-sinners in need of loving guidance. Shepherd her as you need shepherding from above, is the theme here. This is refreshing stuff for the Christian man.

Dennis Gundersen, Senior Pastor, Grace Bible Church, Tulsa Oklahoma, and owner of Grace & Truth Books

Maneuvering your way around society's roadblocks to achieve a God-honoring marriage requires a resource filled with biblical insights and plenty of practical help. Larry McCall provides that and much more in this relational roadmap to happiness, intimacy, and genuine fulfillment. For men who want God's best, this book is like having access to a handheld GPS instead of stopping for directions in the middle of the desert. It's all there! Men who apply the principles of this book stand ready to become culture changers. This may be the best book for men on marriage I have ever read!

Byron Paulus, Chairman of the Board and CEO, Life Action Revival Ministry

Nothing is more important than connecting with men on biblical grounds if we are to turn the tide of marital mediocrity and breakdown. Few authors address husbands without rambling in information overload or falling prey to being condescending and condemning. In this book, Pastor McCall avoids both and effectively mentors the reader, perhaps more effectively than anyone I've read yet.

Paul Spasic, Marriage Ministry Partnerships, Plymouth, Indiana

Many of us are telling men to love the world for Christ's sake. Pastor Larry McCall tells us that we must first learn to love our brides as Christ loves His. The author skirts no issue. Infidelity is sin no matter how well justified. He pulls no punches. A husband may not abuse one he has vowed to protect. And he tells it like it is. Romance and sex can be openly discussed and enjoyed without shame and without timidity when done in the context of God's Word. Pastor McCall makes his book very readable for men who don't read. The only thing that exceeds the number of illustrations is their effectiveness. Although the subject matter will be convicting for every man (there is plenty here for the unmarried man as well), there is an abundance of grace for each of us who will acknowledge our need for it. I am eager to use this text as we equip men to serve the Kingdom of God beyond the walls of the local church. We'll never reach men in the marketplace for Jesus, however, until we learn to love wives in our homes like Jesus loves His bride.

Dr. Bob Shearer, former Executive Director of Men Following Christ, Warsaw, Indiana

Larry McCall's book, *Loving Your Wife as Christ Loved the Church* is a *must read* for any Christian man serous about improving his relationship with his wife! The chapters on "Purifying Love" and "Pardoning Love" are worth the price of the book by themselves. As a leader of more than 50 men's ministries, I believe this book deals with the core issue of a man's loving leadership in the home. It is an excellent resource for the second-year teaching curriculum of Men's Fraternity that we use in our men's ministries. Larry refers the reader to many other excellent resources on the topic as well.

Darryl Sheggrud, Executive Director, Midwest Region, Men's Ministry Network

LOVING YOUR WIFE

As Christ Loves the Church

LOVING YOUR WIFE

As Christ Loves the Church

LARRY E. McCALL

BMH Books
www.bmhbooks.com
Winona Lake, IN 46590

Loving Your Wife As Christ Loves the Church

ISBN: 978-0-88469-304-8
RELIGION / Christian Life / Family

Published by BMH Books
BMH Books, P.O. Box 544, Winona Lake, IN 46590 USA
www.bmhbooks.com

Printed in the United States of America

Interior & Cover design: Terry Julien

Dedication

This book is humbly and gratefully dedicated
to the two greatest loves of my life:

To Gladine

who first captured my heart as a teenager
because of her passion to know Christ
and to make Him known. You are
astonishingly beautiful! Thank you for
saying yes to being my wife since
that wonderful day in 1975.
You are a gift from God to me.

To the Lord Jesus Christ

"who loved me and gave himself for me"
(Galatians 2:20). Your love excels all others.
May You be honored as the men who
read this book reflect the love You have
for Your bride, the church.

Acknowledgments

Even though my name appears on the cover as the author, I humbly recognize that I am only one of many people who have contributed to this book.

In the early 1980s, while my young family and I were attending the Mid-America Reformed Baptist Family Conference in Bluffton, Ohio, I heard Pastor Stu Latimer preach a sermon on "Loving Your Wife as Christ Loves the Church." That planted the seed for this book. Thank you, Stu, for your faithfulness in challenging me as a young husband.

A number of people provided opportunity, time, and a place for writing this book. My thanks go to Terry White and his team at BMH Books for asking me a couple years ago if I was ready to write another book. Their encouragement to me personally to continue to grow in the ministry of writing continues to bear fruit. My precious spiritual family, Christ's Covenant Church of Winona Lake, Indiana, kindly gave me a summer sabbatical in honor of my 25th anniversary as a pastor there, giving me time to research and write. Thank you, church elders and members for your thoughtfulness. My parents-in-law, Chuck and Ruth Rupp, showed their notable hospitality in allowing Gladine and me to live with them in their picturesque summer home along the Allegheny River while I did the bulk of the writing. My much-loved father-in-law has since passed away, and we miss him intensely.

A whole team of sisters in Christ did their best at taking my feeble efforts and improving them through their proofreading and constructive counsel. Kate Harmon, Susan Hight, Kay Finley, and my wife, Gladine, all sacrificed their time to carefully read the first draft. My editor, Joyce K. Ellis, coached me to continue honing my writing, ultimately serving you, the reader, in making this book much more readable. Thank you, sisters!

A number of men close to me also sharpened my thinking on the ministry of husbanding. The four men in my accountability group— Don Clemens, John Urschalitz, Rod Valentine, and Bob Rex—affectionately known as "Old Men for Christ," faithfully challenged and encouraged me during our early Friday breakfast meeting month after month. Thanks, friends. You are faithful brothers indeed. Then, over subs each Friday lunchtime, my own son, David, and sons-in-law, Jake Barros and Josh Armstrong, processed with me the joys and challenges of married life from their generation's perspective. I love you guys, and I'm honored to have you as "sons."

I offer a special word of thanks to my precious wife, Gladine, who, ironically, sacrificed time with me over the past year so I could write this book for husbands who want to better show love to their wives! Lord willing, her sacrifice will benefit not only our own marriage but also the marriages of many men whom the Holy Spirit helps through this book. Thanks, Gladine. I love you.

Most importantly, I humbly acknowledge that all of these precious gifts ultimately have come from the hand of my gracious Lord and Savior. He is good beyond my wildest imagination.

Foreword

We are all inheritors of certain cultural notions—ideas that find their way into common consensus. For example, many men believe that romance is the key to marriage. Books are written to tell us how to stir up a little romance. Men often think they are too practical-minded and need to learn to be a little more romantic and more sensitive to their wives.

In the biblical view, however, worship is the key to marriage. Godly husbanding does not begin with loving your wife; it begins with loving God. The truth that a man should love his wife "as Christ loves the church" is a jewel of truth shining like a diamond in Ephesians 5. In *Loving Your Wife as Christ Loves the Church* Larry McCall lifts this diamond out of the text and through clear, thorough exposition highlights the many facets of what it means to love like Christ.

The reader will find his heart moved to doxology by the incomparable love of Christ for the church. Loving and worshiping God always moves the Christian to love others. McCall has things properly aligned in this excellent little book. His starting point is worship; it is the love of Christ. By emphasizing Christ's love for the church, the author takes our focus off ourselves and our wives and places it on Christ and His undying love for His bride. Various facets of multi-splendored love of Christ for his bride form the basis for the chapters of *Loving Your Wife as Christ Loves the Church*.

While there is great value to seeing the love of Christ as the standard for our calling as husbands, Christ's perfection is quite daunting. Here is where the pastor's heart of Larry McCall shines. His book is full of grace for husbands like me who fail to love as we ought. And it is full of the power and enablement of the gospel. We don't look inside ourselves at our weakness and failure for the strength we need.

To do so simply re-enforces our pride and self-righteousness. This book takes us to Christ for the grace, power, wisdom, understanding, insight, boldness, and courage to love as Christ loved.

Loving Your Wife as Christ Loves the Church is a pleasure to read. It deserves a place as a study book for men's groups. McCall's love for God and his wife, Gladine, is on every page.

Dr. Tedd Tripp, author, conference speaker, and pastor of the Grace Fellowship Church, Hazleton, Pennsylvania

Table of Contents

Introduction

Ryan lifted his gaze from the fraying laces of his running shoes. With a tone I couldn't quite discern (hurt? anger? defensiveness?), Ryan muttered, "But I don't know how to love my wife. I never had a good example. My folks split when I was only nine, and my dad never seemed to have much time for me." In case I hadn't gotten his point the first time, Ryan repeated, "I just don't know how to love my wife. I never had anyone to show me how."

After a few years of marriage that Ryan considered fair, maybe even good, his wife Abby[1] had become sullen and withdrawn—possibly even depressed. One day he had built up enough courage to do some probing. "What's wrong, Abby? You never seem happy anymore."

"I don't know, Ryan," she mumbled. "Being married to you hasn't turned out like I thought it would. You work long days, come home, eat your dinner without saying much, watch TV for hours, crawl into bed after I'm already asleep, then get up the next morning and do the same thing over again. I don't feel loved any longer, Ryan."

He didn't want to, but in desperation, Ryan gave Abby his okay to set up a counseling appointment with me. Now, here they were in their first meeting with me, their pastor. In response to my questions clarifying why they had come, Abby came right out and said, "I don't feel loved by Ryan anymore."

After a few moments of awkward silence, I turned to Ryan and asked, "So, Ryan, do you love her?"

Ryan told me he had loved Abby since they were seniors in high school.

But it was obvious Abby didn't feel loved now. As hard as it was to admit, Ryan knew there was a serious problem with his follow through. But he felt I needed to understand why. Abby needed to understand, too. He had a good reason for not knowing how to show love to his wife.

We men are interesting creatures, aren't we? We tend to gravitate toward those things in which we feel especially competent. Are we good at basketball? Then we tend to make time to play pickup basketball with the guys at the gym or at the asphalt court down the street. We love trash talking the other guy, reminding him how good we are at the sport.

Are we good at mechanical things? Then it's no hardship to spend hours of free time in the garage, puttering with our favorite car or motorcycle.

Fascinated with history? Then we must subscribe to the History Channel, whiling away hours vicariously reliving the wars of bygone generations.

On the other hand, nothing scares us more than having our incompetencies revealed. Better at dribbling your soft drink than a basketball? Watching the playoffs so you can converse with the guys at the water cooler might be all right, but better avoid the gym scene!

Don't know a spark plug from a fireplug? Calling the mechanic to do that repair job is no problem at all.

Think the Desert Fox was an animal? Skip the History Channel. Stick to *Animal Planet*.

Now, as interested as some of us may be in discussing basketball or mechanics or history, let's talk about marriage. Let's talk about *husbanding*. Did you notice the anxiety needle going up a notch or two when you read that word? Why do you suppose that happens? The truth of the matter is that few of us feel competent when it comes to being a husband. And, those who do should probably have a heart-to-heart chat with their wives, getting their honest evaluations!

Since so few of us men feel competent in this area, we tend to shy away from the subject. We don't want our incompetencies exposed. It's safer to talk about our jobs or sports or mechanics or history. So we devote our recreation hours, our TV watching, or our reading time to safer subjects. It's scary for us to talk seriously (rather than joking) about marriage in general and about being husbands in particular. That's why the great majority of couples who attend marriage conferences do so at the initiative (even pleading) of the wife, not the husband. That's why the great majority of books on marriage are purchased by women, not men.

But, you are reading this book, aren't you? And it's for husbands. I commend you. Either on your own initiative or at the encouragement of a trusted friend (maybe even your wife) you have decided to read *Loving Your Wife as Christ Loves the Church*. All married men (and men anticipating marriage) can benefit from reading this book. Whether you just returned from your honeymoon or celebrated your golden wedding anniversary, studying this book will help you find aspects of Christ's love for the church that can shape your love for your wife.

If you are engaged to be married, maybe your pastor or counselor has assigned this book for homework as part of your premarital counseling. I pray that God uses this book to help you bless your soon-to-be wife with Christlike love.

Regardless of where you are on this journey, I would strongly encourage you to quickly skim the table of contents and then lay down the book. Start contacting a few of your married buddies and ask if they would be interested in working through this book together as an accountability group. My hunch is that those who will get the most out of this book will do so as a band of brothers in Christ. If you are interested in starting a men's accountability group but need some pointers, check out Appendix D.

Out of respect for you and your courage to face such a significant topic, I should tell you up front what to expect:

• **This book is Bible-based.** *Loving Your Wife as Christ Loves the Church* is founded on the premise that the institution of marriage is God's invention. The establishment of marriage is not the pragmatic product of any particular culture, or of the society in general. God Himself determined that "It is not good for the man to be alone" (Genesis 2:18). God Himself specifically designed Eve to complete

Adam as his wife. And God Himself performed the first wedding ceremony, presenting Adam's newly formed wife to him, much to his joy (Genesis 2:22–24).

Since God designed marriage, we must depend on His book, the Bible, to explain to us the purposes, roles, and relationships He desires. *Loving Your Wife as Christ Loves the Church,* therefore, is based, not on the ever-changing concepts originating in human-centered psychology or sociology, but on the inerrant, unchanging Word of God.

• **This book is Christ-centered.** In many ways this book is about Him. Even unmarried people are blessed by contemplating how much Jesus Christ loves us, His church. And understanding His love for the church, His bride, is the starting point for each husband to love his wife. Christ is our model. Studying Him and His love for the church is crucial in this ministry of love. If Christ is the model, we are the mirrors. The way you and I mirror Christ in the way we love our wives draws people's attention to our Savior. If anything, this raises the stakes even higher in our husbanding ministry. We don't want to be a bad reflection of Christ to a watching world, do we?

• **This book is grace-promoting.** There's no way we can do this on our own. *Loving Your Wife as Christ Loves the Church* is not a "grit your teeth and just try harder" book. We are totally dependent on the grace of our Lord Jesus Christ in carrying out this awesome ministry of loving our wives. And, praise His name, He gives us the grace to love our wives. "We love, because he first loved us" (1 John 4:19). So if we start feeling hopeless and helpless as we consider afresh all that is involved in loving our wives, we need to pause and look back at the cross. His grace is sufficient for us (2 Corinthians 12:9).

Let's go back to Ryan and Abby's counseling session. With much experience caring for the married couples in our church, I realized that this young husband needed some serious hope. How handicapped was Ryan in never having a father to model godly husbanding? Was Ryan relegated to limping through marriage with a permanent "husband impediment" because of his lack of a godly mentor in his life?

I smiled. "Ryan, I have great news for you. I would like you to have the Mentor of all mentors in your life. He will show you how to love Abby. Let me present to you the Model Husband." With that, I opened my Bible and read, "Husbands, love your wives, just as Christ loved the church and gave himself up for her" (Ephesians 5:25). "Ryan," I said, "in the coming weeks we are going to find the help you need—the help I need—in knowing how to love these precious wives the Lord has given us. We want to learn how to love our wives just as Christ loves the church. Let's learn together from the Perfect Husband."

DISCUSSION QUESTIONS AND ACTION STEPS
Introduction

Discussion Questions*

1. In terms of being a husband, what human role models have you had in your life? In what ways did they impact you positively? Negatively?

2. In what ways do you hope to grow as a husband from reading and discussing this book?

3. Slowly and honestly read through 1 Corinthians 13:4–7, substituting your name for the word *love*. Then answer the following, particularly in regard to your relationship with your wife: Which attributes of love seem foreign when your name is inserted? In what ways might the Lord be calling you to change?

Action Steps

1. Take the first steps toward forming an accountability group. (See Appendix D for ideas on how to start one.) What are some goals and plans you might consider for your group as you read and discuss this book together? For example, when and where will you meet? Do you want to discuss one chapter each time you're together? What rules of confidentiality will you agree on?

2. Pray for yourself and for your group members, asking the Lord to give each of you humility and hope as together you pursue growth in reflecting Christ's love to your wives.

3. Agree on the next meeting time and in what ways you should be prepared for that time together.

---

*If you're studying this on your own or haven't yet formed an accountability group, use these questions and action steps for your own personal reflection and motivation.

1

The Perfect
Husband

It's difficult to do something when you've never been shown how, isn't it? When the stakes are high and the cost of failure is far-reaching, attempting to accomplish an important assignment without having a model to work from can feel overwhelming. And what more important mission does a married man have than being a husband? Do you feel you have a good handle on your responsibility of *husbanding* your wife?

Within hours of signing the contract for writing this book for husbands, feelings of inadequacy overwhelmed me. What had I just signed on for? Although my wife Gladine and I have been married for more than 30 years, I suddenly felt I belonged in the kindergarten class at the school of husbanding. "Lord, show me how to be a husband to this precious daughter of Yours!"

Speaking recently at a conference on the topic of family relationships, I asked the men there, "How many of you grew up in a home with a dad who showed you by his example how to be a godly husband?"

Not surprisingly, only a few of us raised our hands. But I firmly believe that most Christian men want to be the kind of husbands who bring a smile to the face of the Master and who gain the grateful respect of their wives.

But how can we learn? We could use more role models, couldn't we?

Ours is not the first generation to grow up lacking examples of God-pleasing husbanding, however. In the first century, men were converted to Christ out of Greek, Roman, or Jewish backgrounds without much idea at all of how to be the kind of husbands God wanted them to be. God, in His kindness, moved the apostle Paul to write, "Husbands, love your wives, *just as Christ loved the church and gave himself up for her*" (Ephesians 5:25, emphasis added). And by those words, Christian men in all cultures and in all generations were given the same Model. Jesus Christ serves as the Example for husbands everywhere. He is The Perfect Husband.

Great Mystery

Have you ever thought of Jesus as a Husband? Many people probably haven't. After all, He was a bachelor, wasn't He? It's true that during the 33 years Jesus spent physically on this earth, He never married. Yet in Ephesians 5:25–33, Paul pictures Jesus as a Husband and the church as His bride. In fact, in verse 32 Paul says, "This is a profound mystery—but I am talking about Christ and the church." I'm not sure what comes to your mind when you hear the word *mystery*, but that word was used differently in the Bible from the way we use it today in movies and novels. As British pastor D. Martyn Lloyd-Jones explains, "Thank God, the use of the term 'mystery' in the New Testament never carries the idea that it is something which cannot be understood at all. 'Mystery' means something that is inaccessible to the unaided mind. It does not matter how great that mind may be."[1]

So *mystery* doesn't refer to something unknowable, but rather something that will not be known to humans unless God chooses to pull back the curtains and reveal it.

New Testament scholar Harold Hoehner clarifies it this way: A "mystery... is something which was hidden in God and which humans could not unravel by their own ingenuity or study but is revealed by God for all believers to understand."[2]

What was not seen in Old Testament times but has now been revealed by God through the apostle Paul is that Christ is the Husband to His wife, the church. Preacher and author John Piper says, "Marriage is like a metaphor or an image or a picture or a parable or a model that stands for something more than a man and a woman becoming one flesh. It stands for the relationship between Christ and the church. That's the deepest meaning of marriage. It's meant to be a living drama of how Christ and the church relate to each other."[3]

The stakes just got higher. We must study Christ as the Model Husband not only so that we can grow in our own roles and have happier marriages, but also so that we can be better reflectors of Christ. Our marriages, though imperfect, are to be a picture—a living drama—to the watching world of the loving relationship between Christ and the church.

To some degree what the world thinks of Christ and the church will come from what they see in us. They will see how our marriages mirror His relationship with His church as the ultimate marriage prototype. Devoting ourselves to the study of Christ as the Perfect Husband should bear fruit not only in our marriages but also in drawing people's attention to Christ. That's our mission, men!

So what can we learn from Christ, The Perfect Husband?

Foundationally, it is *His love* for His bride. The Holy Spirit could have zeroed in on Christ's authority as Head of the church.[4] That would have been doctrinally legitimate—and may have fed the cravings of power-hungry men! Although Paul mentions the headship of Christ in his counsel to wives in Ephesians 5:23 ("The husband is the head of the wife as Christ is the head of the church"), his directive to husbands draws attention instead to His love for His bride. The implications are significant.

Might it be that God focuses our attention on the dynamic of Christ's love for the church because He knows how much we men need that reminder?

Wielding authority might come naturally to men, but love—the kind of love that Christ demonstrates—must come more deliberately as we choose to follow our Lord, leaning ever so much on His grace. Loving in a Christ-mirroring way goes against the stream of our carnality, requiring us to turn afresh to our Savior for His freely offered grace. And that is just where He wants us—depending on and enjoying His grace in the everyday context of our marriages.

Great Model

In the picture Paul paints in Ephesians 5:25–33, what are some of the most notable characteristics of Christ's love for His bride?

First, the love Christ demonstrates toward the church is *unconditional*. His love for the church is marked by His commitment to do what is best for us even though we never deserved that love. Paul writes, "God demonstrates his own love for us in this: While we were still sinners, Christ died for us" (Romans 5:8). His decision to love us was in no way a response to our love for Him or even to our lovability. The cause of His love is in Himself, not in us.

Second, Christ's love for His bride is profoundly *sacrificial*. How did Peter say it? "You know that it was not with perishable things such as silver or gold that you were redeemed...but with the precious blood of Christ, a lamb without blemish or defect" (1 Peter 1:18).

Author Gary Ricucci notes, "True love is costly. Jesus not only gave what he had—he gave himself."⁵ In the words of the old hymn, we can say, "Amazing love, how can it be, that Thou, my God, shouldst die for me?"⁶

Third, Christ's love for His bride is *voluntary*. Paul's wording in Ephesians 5:25 is picturesque: Jesus "gave himself up for her." The word used for "gave [himself] up" has the idea of "handing over." We could paraphrase the verse this way: "Jesus loved the church and handed himself over for her." No one made Him do it. He took the initiative to pay the price of Himself to purchase His bride.

The night before the cross, Jesus sought to enlighten His disciples about the unconditional, costly, voluntary price He would pay to redeem His church when He said, "Greater love has no one than this, that he lay down his life for his friends" (John 15:13).

Imperfect Mirrors

Two little words in Ephesians 5:25 intimidate me: the words *just as*. "Husbands, love your wives, just as Christ loved the church and gave himself up for her."⁷ How can you and I ever match that kind of love?

Before we give up, deciding the mission we've been given is impossible to carry out, it might be wise to listen to pastor and writer Alistair

Begg, who writes, "While human men cannot match the degree of love Jesus displays (since His love is divine and infinite), they are to love in the same manner."[8] In other words, although we husbands are *imperfect* reflectors of The Perfect Husband, He has commissioned us to love our wives in the same manner as He loves His bride.

- **Loving unconditionally.** Since *His* love is unconditional, *ours* must be also. We will learn more about this in chapter 2, "A Predetermined Love." But let's briefly consider Christ's example that we love our wives without conditions—not held in reserve until we feel loved or respected by our wives, not based on our perception of our wives' lovability, not withholding love until they fix themselves up physically, emotionally, or attitudinally. If, by God's grace, we choose to love our wives irrespective of our perception of their worthiness or responsiveness, we mirror Christ's unconditional love.

- **Loving sacrificially.** Similarly, our Christlike love for our wives should be profoundly sacrificial. While we may hear the occasional story of a husband who literally sacrifices his own life to save his wife's, few of us will be called upon in God's providence to pay that price. However, we make other sacrifices. It is worth our time to consider these heart-searching words from Christian radio host and author Bob Lepine: "It is often harder to live for your wife than it would be to die for her. It involves dying daily to your own desires and dreams. In the end, sacrificial love involves a willingness on the part of a husband not only to prefer his wife as more important than himself (see Philippians 2:3), but a readiness to lay down everything he holds dear to care for her. It is a decision on the part of a husband that nothing will supersede his marriage covenant. It's the kind of love that never gives up."[9]

What evidences of selfishness do I see in my life as a husband? Am I withholding my time, my affection, my words of affirmation and appreciation because I'm not willing to set aside my own priorities? In what ways is the Lord calling me to "die to myself" so that I can better reflect Christ in my sacrificial love for my wife?

- **Loving voluntarily.** Our love must also mirror Christ's voluntary love for His bride. Paltry tokens of love pulled out of us by our desperate wives or pushed out of us by a marriage counselor are less than sufficient. We must continually run back to Christ, soaking in His gracious love for us so that we will be moved to love others—especially our precious wives. Let me paraphrase the Apostle John's words in 1 John 4:19–21: "We love because He first loved us. If anyone says, 'I love God,' yet hates his wife, he is a liar. For anyone who does not love his *wife*, whom he has seen, cannot love God, whom he has not seen. And He has given us this command: Whoever loves God must also love his *wife*."

So, brothers, though we're imperfect, God commissions us to love our wives just as Christ loves His bride, the church. Let's devote ourselves to studying Christ together. Dr. D. Martyn Lloyd-Jones writes, "We must start by studying the relationship between Christ and the church, and then, and then only, can we look at the relationship between the husband and the wife."[10]

Let's begin our journey. Each of the following chapters explores one quality of Christ's love for His bride and ways in which we, though imperfect mirrors, can better reflect The Perfect Husband.

DISCUSSION QUESTIONS AND ACTION STEPS
The Perfect Husband

Discussion Questions

1. What aspects of being a husband seem to come easiest to you?

2. What do you think are some of the most challenging aspects of being a husband? What part of being a husband is especially difficult for you personally?

3. What attributes of Jesus' love for His bride, the church, especially grip you? Why?

4. What particular characteristics of Christ's love would you like for your non-Christian friends and relatives to see as they watch you relate to your wife?

Action Steps

1. Pray for humility in learning to become more Christlike in your love for your wife. Then do the following:

2. Being careful to avoid becoming defensive, ask your wife in what ways she would like to see you grow as a husband. Ask her if she would commit to praying for you each day as you seek to grow in your ministry of being a Christlike husband.

2

A Predetermined Love

"To have and to hold, from this day forward, for better for worse, for richer for poorer, in sickness and in health, to love and to cherish, till death do us part." I was only 21 years old, but those were the vows I made to my even younger bride that June day more than 30 years ago. Maybe you made the same or similar vows.

Author and speaker Jim George asks us a thought-provoking question:

> In the months or years since that day [of your wedding], have you thought back on the vows you made to your bride? When was the last time you thought about your vows and the commitments you made? I'm sure, if you're like most men, the last time you thought about the wedding ceremony was on the day of your wedding. What's ironic about our tendency to forget about our vows is that our wedding day is one of the most important occasions in our life. What we say at that ceremony affects us for the rest of our lives.[1]

Have you ever counted how many *ifs* there are in the traditional wedding vows? You know, "I promise today to love you *if* you continue to consistently treat me in a way that makes me feel good about myself" or "I promise to love you today *if* you keep your attractive figure after bearing three children."

Count them. How many *ifs* did you say in your wedding vows? That's right. Zero. And that's the way it's supposed to be. On your wedding day and mine, each of us made a solemn promise to our bride in the presence of God and the gathered witnesses that we would love our wives no matter what. That's what "for better for worse, for richer for poorer, in sickness and in health" means. No *ifs*. The husband, in a sense, tells his bride and all witnessing that sacred event that he decided ahead of time that he would love his wife no matter what would happen in the future. Have you ever thought about that regarding your wife?

On the wedding day there is no way of knowing what the future holds—what changes, challenges, hardships lie ahead.

Nevertheless, we pledge our faithful love. We pledge a "predetermined" love—a "decided-ahead-of-time" love that does not quit when those changes and challenges come.

Christ's Deliberate Choice

When did the Lord decide to love us?

Did He choose to love us after some probationary period in our Christian experience—after seeing that maybe we would make an okay bride for Him after all? No. His love preceded that. Otherwise, He might never have loved us!

Did He decide to love us on the day of our salvation? No. His decision to love us predated that day.

Did He decide to love us on the day He watched us being born? No. He decided long before that.

The Bible says, "He chose us in him before the creation of the world to be holy and blameless in his sight. In love he predestined us to be adopted as his sons through Jesus Christ, in accordance with his pleasure and will—to the praise of his glorious grace" (Ephesians 1:4–6). Think of it!

Even before uttering those words recorded in Genesis 1:3, "Let there be light!" God had already decided to love us. Christ's love for us, His bride, is a decided-ahead-of-time love. His love is a predetermined love. No conditions. No *ifs*.

Bob Lepine says it this way:

> His love for us is not based in any way on how we will perform.
> He does not find us attractive because, as some have suggested,

he looks down the corridors of time and is drawn to those who would one day choose to follow him. No, according to the Scripture, there is only one reason why God chose us to be his adopted sons. It is because it was 'the kind intention of His will, to the praise of the glory of His grace' (Ephesians 1:5–6 NASB). To put it another way, God chose us as his adopted sons because he wanted to. Pure and simple.[2]

We could go even further than saying the Lord's love for us, His bride, doesn't depend on our worthiness. Way back before the creation of the world, when our omniscient God decided to love us, He was very aware that we would, in fact, be unworthy of His love. Paul put it this way: "You see, at just the right time, when we were still powerless, Christ died for the ungodly. Very rarely will anyone die for a righteous man, though for a good man someone might possibly dare to die. But God demonstrates his own love for us in this: While we were still sinners, Christ died for us" (Romans 5:6–8).

Speaking to the congregation at Westminster Chapel, Dr. Martyn Lloyd-Jones clarified this truth. "He loved us, not because of anything in us; he loved us in spite of what was in us, 'while we were yet sinners'. He loved the ungodly, 'while we were yet enemies'. In all our unworthiness and vileness He loved us. He loved the church, not because she was glorious and beautiful—no, but that He might make her such."[3]

The Bible is clear. His was a predetermined love—an unconditional love—a no-matter-what kind of love. No *ifs*: "Husbands, love your wives, just as Christ loved the church and gave himself up for her" (Ephesians 5:25).

Lepine reminds us, "A husband who would love his wife as Christ also loved the church will begin by understanding that his love is a choice, made in spite of (not because of) his wife's actions, attitudes or appearance. Once he has called her to be his wife, a husband makes a pledge of unconditional love for his wife, for better or worse."[4]

For Better For Worse

It is so humbling to think about how often over the years I have responded to my wife, Gladine, because I thought she loved me, respected me, or supported my leadership. When I have felt loved and honored, I have showered my love on her. When I have not felt the love and support I desired, I have withheld my expressions of love. How un-Christlike! More often than I would care to remember, my love has been conditional. There have been way too many *ifs*.

Yet on that warm June day long ago, I vowed my predetermined love for her. I promised her that I had already decided to love her "as long as we both shall live," no matter what. And my beautiful blue-eyed bride was not the only one listening attentively to my vows that day. So was my God. "When you make a vow to God, do not delay in fulfilling it," Solomon wrote. "He has no pleasure in fools; fulfill your vow. It is better not to vow than to make a vow and not fulfill it" (Ecclesiastes 5:4–5).

How kind God has been in not treating *me* as my sins deserve (Psalm 103:10) but loving me unconditionally because of the cross of Christ. He is gracious beyond my wildest imaginations. May I mirror the love of my Lord as I minister to my wife with a predetermined love, not only in the good times but even in the less-than-enjoyable seasons of our marriage.

It might mean loving her unconditionally through the irritability that can come at certain times during the month. It might mean loving her unilaterally during seasons of discouragement or depression when she's not sure *she* loves *me*. It might even mean loving her determinedly with a Hosea-like love through periods when she may be living in rebellion against the Lord who bought her.[5]

For Richer For Poorer

Seasons of financial struggle can take a toll on any marriage. There is only so much money to go around, and the husband may have a very different idea about how to use that money than his wife has. These arguments can rip and tear at marriages. Frustrated husbands may pressure and pout, leaving their wives feeling anything but loved. Selfish husbands who ignore their wives' priorities and pleas leave those precious women feeling disrespected and unloved. The "for poorer" seasons of life can test a man's love for his wife. But if we have decided ahead of time to love our wives in an unconditional, Christlike way, God's grace will see us through.

Many men may be eagerly waiting for their love to be tested during the "richer" periods, thinking that being richer would make things more pleasant in their marriages. Yet riches can bring their own strain if they are not handled in a God-honoring way.

Speaking from experience, no doubt, the writer of Ecclesiastes confessed, "Whoever loves money never has money enough; whoever loves wealth is never satisfied with his income. This too is meaningless" (5:10).

A bigger income doesn't guarantee a happier marriage. Riches themselves can test priorities and loyalties. If God decides to entrust to us more than we need, we must remember our predetermined love for our wives. Our earthly loyalty should be to her, not to our money and things. We must always see her and love her as "worth far more than rubies" (Proverbs 31:10).

In Sickness and in Health

Few men who marry young, as I did, give this vow much thought as they prepare for marriage. Yet as the years wear on, our bodies wear down. Will the bride who participated in strenuous recreational activities with us or who enjoyed passionate physical intimacy with us in our youth find us just as loving when she needs her walker to get around or when she struggles through the fog of Alzheimer's to show us the simplest of affections?

If a wife's health fails before his, it is so tempting, in our what's-in-it-for-me? culture, for a husband to justify himself in finding some other object for his affections. But if we have come to grips with the Lord's grace and the Lord's directive to love our wives just as Christ loves the church, then we will love her through any debilitating illnesses or the ravages of old age. Some of us have seen husbands who have modeled this for us: One man verbally reassures his wife of his undying love for her as he tenderly washes and clothes her body that is progressively degenerating from MS. Another daily visits the nursing home, spoon-feeding his Alzheimer's-devastated wife while singing to her the love songs of their youth. A Christlike predetermined love will see us through all the seasons of marriage—in sickness and in health.

To Love and to Cherish, Till Death Do Us Part

Christ loves us with a predetermined love. His reason for loving us is not based on conditions in us, His bride. There are no *ifs*. We can count on His predetermined love, not having to live in fear that He will capriciously change His mind one day because of something *we* have done or neglected to do. His reason for loving us lies wholly within Himself, not within us. He has already decided and promised to love us without end. "Never will I leave you; never will I forsake you" (Heb. 13:5).

Can my wife live with a similar assurance that I have decided and promised to love her no matter what? To love and to cherish her, till death us do part? Many years ago, on that warm June day, she heard me make that vow. I promised to love her with a predetermined love until the Lord calls one or both of us home. No *ifs*.

DISCUSSION QUESTIONS AND ACTION STEPS
A Predetermined Love

Discussion Questions

1. Why does God love you? What would it take for the Lord to stop loving someone? On what passages from the Bible would you base your answer?

2. Read through Ephesians 1:3–14. In this passage what grips you and why?

3. How much of your wedding vows can you still recall?

4. What specifically do you love about your wife? Are these things in any way "conditions" for you to continue to love her? What if she stops being that way or doing those things that have prompted your affection? Would your love for her continue?

Action Steps

1. Surprise your wife this week by arranging time for the two of you to sit on the couch, leisurely looking at your wedding album together.

2. Remind her (as best you can remember) of your wedding vows to her on that day. Tell her that you meant those vows then and you still mean them today!

3

A Peerless Love
Part 1

Jesus loves everybody in the world: Do you agree or disagree? It's so easy to say, "Yes, He does." In fact, disagreeing might invite the label of *heretic*. In one sense, it is true that God loves everybody. "He causes his sun to rise on the evil and the good, and sends rain on the righteous and the unrighteous" (Matthew 5:45). God really does care about all His creatures, especially His special image bearers, human beings. He shows that Creator-love by providing air and food and life itself.

But does the Lord love everyone in the same way? Or, does He have a particular love—a preferential love for some people?

Jesus' Peerless Love for His Bride

To look for an answer to that intriguing question, let's eavesdrop on Jesus' conversation with His heavenly Father the night before the cross. People have often noted that a man's true heart is most clearly heard in the words he utters as He is about to die. So what was on Jesus' heart in those hours before the cross? *Who* was on Jesus' heart? The apostle John heard Jesus pray: "I have revealed you to those whom you gave me out of the world. They were yours; you gave them to me...I pray for them. I am not praying for the world, but for those you have given me" (John 17:6, 9).

Interesting, isn't it? Just hours before the cross, Jesus distinguishes those who were His from those He refers to as "the world."[1]

God the Father chose this group of people in eternity past and gave them to the Son to redeem. Although Jesus surely had a general love for all people, He indicated a preferential love for this particular group—"His people." Shouldn't this have a profound implication on our understanding of the passage, "Husbands, love your wives, just as Christ loved the church and gave himself up for her" (Ephesians 5:25)?

Jesus confirms His focused, special love for His people, the church, by the way He treats His bride—in ways He does not treat the mass of humanity in general. Not every individual in the world has been redeemed.

However, the Bible records that He gave Himself for them, the people of His special love, redeeming them through His work on the cross. And, as we will see in subsequent chapters, Jesus is not some fickle "love 'em and leave 'em" husband. No, He continues to show His *peerless* love for His Bride by sticking with us, persistently molding us, so that we might become "a radiant church without stain or wrinkle or any other blemish, but holy and blameless" (Ephesians 5:27).

He has lovingly given us everything we need for life and godliness (2 Peter 1:3). All the love He has poured out uniquely on His church is with that glorious goal in view—the ultimate wedding day between Him and His bride, the church (Ephesians 5:27; Revelation 19:9; 21:2). Truly our heavenly Husband has *lavished* His love upon us (1 John 3:1). How can we help but feel overwhelmed with the peerless, dedicated love He has for us as His bride.

Our Peerless Love for Our Wives

If we husbands are going to love our wives just as Christ loved the church, we must do our best to help them feel our special, preferential love—that there is no other thing, no other activity, no other person on this earth who matters more to us than they. Our wives should feel unquestionably cherished by us. As Pastor Alistair Begg says, "There is no more precious gift entrusted to a man than the treasure of his wife. She is to be admired and prized above all others. She is to have first place in his heart, mind, and affections. She is to be given special care and attention that leaves no doubt of her husband's esteem."[2]

I think a literal translation of 1 Timothy 3:2 may serve us well here. In giving necessary qualifications for an overseer in the church, Paul includes this: The overseer must be...[literally] a one-woman man. This term also has been translated as "the husband of but one wife" (NIV) or "the husband of one wife" (ESV, KJV, NASB).

What is Paul getting at? It is highly unlikely that Paul is addressing the issue of whether divorced, remarried men—or widowed, remarried men—can become elders in the church. While that might be an issue for churches to tackle, I think it misses the point of 1 Timothy 3. Paul is primarily dealing with character issues.

He's saying that if an overseer/elder is going to model the normal Christian life for the other men in the church, he needs to be a one-woman man. Marital infidelity ran rampant in the Roman Empire when Paul wrote even as it does in our culture today. The church needed leaders who modeled unquestionable loyalty to their wives— men who showed their wives that special, peerless love for them and them alone.

Ears for Her Alone

As a boy growing up in the hills of western Pennsylvania, I once went raccoon hunting with some friends under the supervision of the men from my home church's unit of The Christian Service Brigade, an evangelical boys ministry. Raccoon hunting takes place with the help of dogs ─at night! After all, raccoons are nocturnal creatures.

Raccoon dogs are trained to sniff out the trail of one of the unfortunate furry creatures, chasing it until the raccoon is "treed." The dogs bay a mournful, wailing bark during the chase. Then when the hunted critter is up a tree (literally), the baying changes, signaling the hunter that the quarry is available for the kill or for release.

On this memorable first raccoon-hunting experience, I heard the baying of a dog named Blue get farther and farther away until it became nearly imperceptible. In our inexperienced concern for this hunting dog, my teenage friends and I began shouting into the dark woods ahead of us, "Here, Blue! Here, Blue! Come here, Blue!"

Nothing.

In desperation, with flashlights in hand, we found our way to the wizened old hunter, Mr. Bowser (no kidding), who owned Blue. We told him our concern.

He gave a simple shout, "Yo, Blue!" In a little while we could hear the rustle of leaves in the dark woods. Soon, tail wagging, Blue came panting up to Mr. Bowser.

Incredulous, we Daniel Boone wannabes asked the old hunter, "How did you do that?"

His answer was simple. "Well, old Blue is a one-man dog."

A one-man dog. Hmm. In other words, we boys could have shouted our lungs out all night and old Blue never would have responded. He had ears for just one man, his owner, Mr. Bowser. Old Blue responded to one voice and one voice alone.

Do I have ears for one woman alone or am I easily influenced by another woman's flattery or come-ons? Am I a one-woman man? Are you? Is all of me dedicated to one woman and one woman only? How about my thoughts? My affections?

Eyes for Her Alone

How about my eyes? Are my eyes dedicated to one woman alone?

One day when I was at the mall with my wife, we walked by the Victoria's Secret store, its windows full of enticement. Gladine passionately implored, "Don't look!"

Why was her plea so emphatic? She wants me to have eyes for her alone. She doesn't want me gawking—or even taking a surreptitious second look—at another woman's body. Our wives want to know we are enraptured with them and them alone. They long to feel our unique, dedicated love so we can say to them with integrity, "How beautiful you are, my darling! Oh, how beautiful!" (Song of Songs 1:15). "Just looking" at other women, whether at the mall, the beach, or on the Internet can seem so innocent, so excusable. After all, what harm is there in a little look?

However, our eyes are the gates to our souls, and a look becomes lust at light speed. Lust is never satisfied, constantly nagging at our hearts and bodies for more, more, more! Soon, those eyes that were dedicated to our wives alone lustfully ogle other women.

Some time ago, a married couple came into my study, asking for counsel. When I asked why they came, the wife said she had discovered some pornography hidden away in their home.

The husband quickly offered a casual defense. "I don't see the big deal. It's not hurting anyone." Since he was looking in my direction, and not at his wife, he didn't see the tears streaming down her cheeks.

I'm sure a bit of "Irish ire" tinged my reply. "Look at your wife!" I insisted. "Look at her! Do you see those tears streaming down her face? How can you say that it's not hurting anyone?"

As any honest wife would, this wife confessed to feeling cheapened and defrauded, just thinking about her husband preferring to look at the bodies of other women over hers, or considering that he may have been fantasizing about those air-brushed, pornographically posed models even while using her body for surrogate sex.

I'm sad to say that despite our attempts to redeem this marriage, it ended in divorce. The husband had grossly underestimated the impact of "just looking." No big deal? Not harming anyone? He crushed the heart of his wife, to whom he had pledged his unique love. In his vain attempt to satisfy the insatiable lust of his heart, fueled by his sinful pornography habit, he sacrificed his marriage.

This man certainly is not alone. Author and radio preacher Chuck Swindoll candidly observes, "Non-Christians and Christians alike wrestle with [lust's] presence and its persistence throughout their lives. Some think that getting married will cause temptation to flee. It doesn't…But sensual imagination goes with them, fighting and clawing for attention and gratification,…Temptation is there, relentlessly pleading for satisfaction."[3]

So, what can the Christian husband do to make sure that his "eyes" are for his wife, and for her alone?

1. Consider the seriousness of "the lust of the eyes" (1 John 2:16). Looking lustfully at another woman at work or at the beach or on the hotel's TV or on the Internet is not an innocent pastime. It is an offense against the God who bought us with the precious blood of His Son. A refusal to flee sexual temptation of any kind, but instead lingering on it, is an act of disobedience. The Bible says explicitly,

You know what instructions we gave you by the authority of the Lord Jesus. It is God's will that you should be sanctified; that you should avoid sexual immorality; that each of you should learn how to control his own body in a way that is holy and honorable, not in passionate lust like the heathen, who do not know God... Therefore, he who rejects this instruction does not reject man but God, who gives you his Holy Spirit (1 Thessalonians 4:2–5, 8).

Consider the damage done by entertaining lust—not only to your relationship with God but also to your own soul. Dietrich Bonhoeffer, the German theologian who gave his life in resisting Hitler, wrote this powerfully personal description of lust:

In our members there is a slumbering inclination towards desire which is both sudden and fierce. With irresistible power, desire seizes mastery over the flesh. All at once a secret, smouldering fire is kindled. The flesh burns and is in flames...Joy in God is...extinguished in us and we seek all our joy in the creature. At this moment God is quite unreal to us....Satan does not here fill us with hatred of God, but with forgetfulness of God....The lust thus aroused envelops the mind and will of man in deepest darkness. The powers of clear discrimination and of decision are taken from us....It is here that everything within me rises up against the Word of God.[4]

Over time, habitual lust can lead a man—even a married man—to forgo reality and instead prefer the cheap substitute of a fantasy world. In his preoccupation with lustful fantasies, the man's soul becomes increasingly desensitized to satisfaction with the real pleasures of marital love. John Ensor writes, "In pornography, love is idealized as sexual satisfaction without intimacy, friendship, or obligations. It is not real."[5]

2. *Consider the damage to the heart of your wife and your relationship with her.* Even if you are somehow able to keep your illusionary world secret from your wife, the marriage will be affected. Your desire for your wife will be diluted. No longer will she enjoy that

unique, dedicated love due her and her alone. Often, men who covertly indulge in pornography also secretly satisfy themselves sexually through masturbation. And this practice robs his wife of what is hers alone, the full possession of his body for her sexual satisfaction (1 Corinthians 7:4–5).

3. *Realizing the damage done, repent of the sin of failing to flee the temptation, which leads to entertaining lust.* True repentance involves both verbal confession of the sin and actually turning away from it. "He who conceals his sins does not prosper, but whoever confesses and renounces them finds mercy" (Proverbs 28:13).

When confessing the sin to the Lord, call it what it is. It is not merely a problem. It is not a disorder. It is a sin. And the Apostle John writes, "If we confess our sins, he is faithful and just and will forgive us our sins and purify us from all unrighteousness" (1 John 1:9). There is forgiveness in Christ!

4. *Get serious about your repentance.* In grateful repentance, do what it takes to get rid of unnecessary temptations. In his book, *Point Man,* Steve Farrar writes, "I can promise you this: If we don't get extreme with the temptation of our eyes, then it will get extreme with us."[6] He's right, isn't he? Speaking in attention-grabbing hyperbole, Jesus says, "If your right eye causes you to sin, gouge it out and throw it away. It is better for you to lose one part of your body than for your whole body to be thrown into hell" (Matthew 5:29).

What do you need to "gouge out and throw away?" I have a friend who, while traveling on business, asks the hotel maintenance people to remove the TV from his room to lessen his temptation to lust. Other men may need to put a pornography blocker on their computers, asking their wives or an accountability partner to check on them. Some of these drastic measures may feel awkward, but we must have eyes for our wives alone.

I recall a visit my wife and I made to Florida. We were visiting a particularly popular beach during spring break. There were many young women on the beach in less-than-modest swimsuits. After a few minutes I confessed to Gladine that I was struggling with my eyes. We came up with a creative solution: We asked some locals if there were other beaches nearby that were frequented primarily by retirees or families instead of college students. Going to another beach not only benefited my soul but also encouraged my precious wife. She appreciated my openness regarding the struggle with my eyes.

5. *Ask the Lord for His help.* Maybe we should make this step number two—or one! Craig Peters writes,

> For most of us it [dealing with sexual lust] is an everyday (maybe every hour or every minute) battle to keep lustful passions under control. The long process it takes for a man to be delivered from the internal war with sexual passions is neither easy nor pleasant, and most certainly it will stretch our relationships for a time. Why is it that when all our resources are diminished, all of our options are spent, and we are lost with little or no idea of how to get home, we finally push our male ego aside and resort to prayer?[7]

Our Lord understands. He cares. He can help. "For we do not have a high priest who is unable to sympathize with our weaknesses, but we have one who has been tempted in every way, just as we are—yet was without sin. Let us then approach the throne of grace with confidence, so that we may receive mercy and find grace to help us in our time of need" (Hebrews 4:15–16).

6. *By God's gifts of mercy and grace commit to fighting the war against lust.* Job, a married man, openly revealed his own battle when he told his friends, "I made a covenant with my eyes not to look lustfully at a girl" (Job 31:1). Not a bad idea, is it? With full dependence on God's grace, it would be wise for each of us to make such a covenant with our eyes. If we take seriously the sinfulness of sin, and if we long for the glory of God to be reflected through our lives as sons of the High King of heaven, we will gladly make such a resolution, giving the lust of the eyes no residence in our lives.

7. *Build into your life encouraging accountability relationships.* The Lord designed the Christian life to be lived in the context of community. We walk this journey with our brothers and sisters in Christ, helping each other along the way.[8] Yet so many Christian men

struggle in isolation with their lustful temptations. How beneficial it would be if we would humble ourselves before God and before our brothers in Christ, admitting our struggles and asking them to keep us accountable.

For years I have benefited personally from participation in a men's accountability group. Nearly every Friday morning for the past five years, four men from our church and I have gathered at a local restaurant for the purpose of helping one another live for Christ in our personal lives, our homes, our church, and our community. We can ask each other anything and freely share our struggles without fear of condemnation.

If you are not currently in this kind of relationship with other Christian brothers, I highly recommend that you join or form such a group. (See Appendix D.)

In addition, we need to share our temptation struggles and the confession of our sins with our dear wives, the person closest to us on this earth.[9]

Lips for Her Alone

A Christian husband committed to being a one-woman man will discover that conversations can get us into trouble sometimes too. How can we talk to other women in a manner that reassures our wives that our lips belong to them alone?

Compliments

In my ministry I converse with hundreds, if not thousands, of people during the course of a year. And as a pastor I find myself wanting to make encouraging comments to people I meet in the church lobby and those who greet me after I've spoken at a conference or another church.

So one seemingly innocent issue I've wrestled with is whether or not to compliment a woman on her appearance. Should I, as a husband, ever say to a woman, "My, but you look nice today!" or "You fixed your hair differently. Looks great!"?

Over the years, I've established a personal policy never to compliment a woman on her physical appearance unless she is my mother, my daughter, or my wife. The only exception I can recall is if a woman is old enough to be my mother and her "glow" as an elderly sister in Christ deserves an encouraging word.

Otherwise, I have resolved to remain mum regarding the physical appearance of any woman outside my immediate family. On those rare occasions when a woman is naively (or maybe intentionally) fishing for a compliment from me, I have responded with a pointed politeness, saying something like this: "I think I will defer to my wife on that!"

I believe we married men should avoid not only speaking *to* other women about their physical appearance, but we should also avoid speaking *about* the physical appearance of women other than our wives. What must my wife feel in her heart if I make a comment such as this: "Wow! Jennifer looks great after losing that extra weight"? Or what if, while watching TV, I say, "Now, there's a babe!"? It would surely make Gladine's heart sink to realize my lips were not dedicated to complimenting her alone on physical beauty.

My foolish words also tell her that I have not dedicated my *eyes* to her alone either. I've been looking at the body of another woman in an approving way. My wife would probably be hurt, assuming I'm comparing her to the other woman and she has just lost this impromptu "beauty pageant."

Flirting

An even more dangerous habit of the lips is flirting with women other than our wives. Some men think it a sport to flirt with female coworkers, women at the fitness center, or even women at church. But it's a dangerous game. A little friendly teasing can lead to even friendlier conversations. Eventually these seemingly serendipitous encounters in the break room or at the fitness center turn into intentionally planned meetings.

Steve Farrar warns, "The problem with getting together and talking is this: The woman will be interested in what you have to say. As you discuss your ideas and plans, you will undoubtedly find her to be encouraging. You will begin to sense an attitude of understanding and appreciation that perhaps you haven't gotten at home recently."[10]

Soon you may find yourself enjoying talking to this other woman even more than you enjoy talking to your wife, compromising your dedicated love for her. In addition, the other woman can easily be enticed into sinful feelings for you, a married man. Your own wife will be hurt, and so will the other woman's husband—if she's married.

Avoid flirting. Don't do it. Paul's counsel to Timothy is just as helpful to us today as it was then: "Treat…younger women as sisters, with absolute purity" (1 Timothy 5:2).

Dedicate your lips to your wife, and to her alone. Heap words of encouragement and compliments on her. Tell her what you enjoy about her hair or her eyes or her lips (and so on down her body!). Need ideas? Read the Song of Solomon, making Solomon's analogies culturally appropriate, of course! Assure her of your peerless love for her by how you speak of her physical attractiveness—and how you *don't* speak of the physical attractiveness of other women. Let her know that your lips are hers, and hers alone.

Hands for Her Alone

"To hug, or not to hug," that is the question. It's so easy to defend liberal hugging between the sexes with "That's just the way we _____ [fill in with your ethnic background] are!" or "We're just a "hugging church!" While I would like to accept those rationalizations, I think we need some words of caution regarding physical touch between a man and a woman who aren't married to each other.

1. *Consider the heart of this woman who is not your wife.* As men respond sexually to sight, women respond to touch. It's possible that the man is trying to communicate nothing beyond a friendly greeting, but, if the woman is starved for male attention, your physical touch could draw her in an improper direction.

I recall a very uncomfortable situation in our church a few years back. Between worship services, a woman close to my age began pouring out her heart concerning her very recent breakup with her husband. She was crying and looked like she needed a hug. Despite the sympathy the Lord had placed in my heart for this hurting woman, I felt a "gut check" that I was not the right person to give the needed hug. I looked around for my wife, but not seeing her at the moment, I spied a nearby sister in the Lord. "Cindy," I said, "I think Susan needs a hug. Would you be so kind?"[11] The physical comfort Susan needed came much more appropriately from a sister in the Lord, and not some married man (me)! When my wife heard about this incident later, she thanked me for handling it that way. She needs to know that my "hands"—my physical touches—are hers alone.

2. *Consider your own heart.* We men enjoy a woman's admiration and appreciation. But a woman's "positive" response to your physical touches may draw your own heart toward her and away from your wife. If the warning lights start going off on the dashboard of your life, back off! Don't just walk away. Run away!

But aren't there times when a brotherly hug is appropriate? Maybe. But use caution. My personal policy is to avoid hugging women outside my family unless my wife is right beside me, and she has already hugged this lady. If this other woman is married, and you feel close as couples, a brotherly hug of both him and her may be appropriate. Without becoming legalistic, this simple advice can prevent potential problems: When in doubt, don't.

Steve Farrar echoes this counsel. "There's nothing wrong with a hug," he writes. "But the next time you think about hugging a woman, and you're not sure about your motives, don't. If you want to hug somebody, go find your wife."[12] Better to err on the side of caution, not only to guard our own susceptible hearts, but also to reassure our wives that our touch is for her, and her alone.

Am I such a one-woman man that my wife unquestionably feels I am solely dedicated to her? Through our daily conversation and actions, let's assure our wives that they are clearly the objects of our special peerless love so they don't need to fear any competition.

DISCUSSION QUESTIONS AND ACTION STEPS
A Peerless Love (Part 1)

Discussion Questions

1. What part of this chapter, "A Peerless Love," especially gripped you and why?

2. What qualities of Jesus' love for "His people" differ from His love for the whole world? (See John 17:6–26.)

3. Read Proverbs 6:20–35. What are some consequences of giving in to sexual sin?

4. What boundaries have you set up in your life to guard your eyes from various forms of pornography so that your wife can be assured that your eyes are for her alone?

5. If a man is committed to reflecting Christ, how should he treat women to whom he's not married? (See 1 Timothy 5:2.)

Actions Steps

1. Can you identify a time or times when you have compromised your commitment to a peerless love for your wife by being too friendly with another woman (or other women)? Confess that to the Lord right now. In what ways is the Holy Spirit calling you to repent? What steps do you need to take?

2. What changes in your daily life should you consider in order for your wife to feel reassured of your peerless love for her? Remember the various topics covered in this chapter: ears, eyes, lips and hands. How might you demonstrate to your wife that you are a one-woman man in each of these areas? Humbly ask for her input.

3. In what aspects of a peerless love for your wife is the Holy Spirit convicting you? Will you humbly confess those to the Lord and commit to repenting of them right now? Talk to the other guys in your group, asking for prayer support and accountability.

4

A Peerless Love
Part 2

Greg sat there in my office, shifting in his chair and looking at the floor with an occasional upward glance at me. It was a difficult conversation for both of us but especially for him. He had become involved sexually with a woman who was not his wife. By God's mercy he had come under great conviction of his sin. And as he confessed it to me, I must have fallen into a stunned silence for a few moments. I had considered him a godly man. The woman he had been involved with was highly regarded in our church as a godly woman.

Finally he broke the awkward silence. "I guess we just didn't see it coming," he said.

And I responded, "I guess that was a big part of the problem, wasn't it?"

A Heart for Her Alone

I doubt many professing Christian men sit around scheming ways to break their wedding vows. I've heard more than one man caught in adultery say, "I don't know what happened. I guess we just fell in love.'"

I don't wish to be unkind, but there *were* warning signs. Somehow these men had ignored one warning light after another on the dashboard of their lives. But how does a married man, who has pledged his unrivaled love to his wife, end up sharing his heart (and his body) with another woman?

Steve Farrar in *Point Man* describes the way adulterous affairs can grow out of the soil of dissatisfaction at home:

It usually begins with discontent. Things have changed. It's not the way it used to be between the two of you....You don't seem to have the same good times you had when you were dating. You rarely enjoy good conversation. You're just not close. You eat at the same table, share the same bathroom, sleep in the same bed, but you might as well be hundreds of miles apart."[1]

But rather than taking initiative to address the growing distance between him and his wife, the husband begins to wonder quietly if he should have married her in the first place. By default, if not by design, the discontented husband is setting himself up for disaster.

In *Lasting Love* Alistair Begg comments, "It's eye-opening to hear how often an extramarital affair begins with casual conversation around the water cooler, while having coffee together, or in some other 'innocent' arena. Yet any time one person takes a discussion into new levels of intimacy beyond what he or she shares with a spouse, the weed sprouts and begins to bloom."[2]

Often in those "casual conversations" that Pastor Begg alludes to, one or both parties slip in some comment about things not being great at home:

"My wife [or husband] just doesn't understand me." The hook was just dropped in the water. Soon one or the other adds *the barb* to the hook of discontent: "My wife [or husband] just doesn't understand me—*like you do.*"

Then the barbed hook gets the bait: "Want to get together and talk about it? It sounds like we have a lot in common right now."

The caution lights of the man's conscience are urgently blinking their warning: "Run away! Run away!" Tragically, in his discontent and his desire to satisfy the loneliness of his soul (and/or the lustful raging of his body), he ignores his conscience and begins to rationalize: "I'm so unsatisfied in my marriage right now. Surely God wants me to be happy, and I feel happier around this other woman than I have felt in ages. What harm is there in just getting together to talk? Anyway, there's no reason my wife even needs to know about it."

So begin the meetings with this other woman. They go from chance encounters to planned trysts. Within days or weeks the man finds that emotionally (if not physically—yet) he has swallowed the hook of adultery, and he's not sure if he even wants to spit it out.

Before long he gives his heart and body to another woman, sinfully violating the promise he made to his wife on their wedding day.

If You've Been Hooked

Are you in an adulterous relationship? Maybe you've been found out and that's why you are reading this book. Maybe you think your sin is still concealed, but you're scared. You're looking for a way out before it's too late. What should you do?

1. Call your relationship with this other woman what God calls it in His Word—adultery. In *What Makes a Man?*, edited by Bill McCartney, who founded Promise Keepers, Steve Farrar writes a chapter, entitled, "Real Men Don't." He emphasizes the importance of properly identifying this sin.

> There's something strange about this epidemic other than its rolling virtually unchecked through the body of Christ. What is strange is that we don't call it "adultery." Let's cut the double talk. Let's put the cards on the table. Let's call adultery what it is. In the way of the family, adultery is treason. But we don't call it treason. We have developed a more refined and sophisticated term. Adultery has become an "affair."[3]

The habit of using a term like *affair* instead of *adultery* tends to soften, in our minds, its offensiveness to God. But if you long to be drenched in the marvel of God's forgiving mercy and grace, don't fool yourself into thinking what you've done is not so bad. Minimizing your sin minimizes your need for His grace. And it minimizes your appreciation of His glory. How does that benefit you?

"Own" your sin. Make no excuses. Avoid all blame shifting. Cry out to God with the confession of King David when he was hooked by adultery: "Have mercy on me, O God, according to your unfailing love; according to your great compassion blot out my transgressions. Wash away all my iniquity and cleanse me from my sin. For I know my transgressions, and my sin is always before me. Against you, you only, have I sinned and done what is evil in your sight" (Psalm 51:1–4).[4]

2. *Confess your sin to those with whom you are spiritually accountable,* such as your wife, your pastors, and your accountability partners. Be transparent. James commands it. "Confess your sins to each other and pray for each other so that you may be healed" (5:16). As scary as this might be to you, you will ultimately be stronger in your fight against sin if you *confess* your sin to other members of the body of Christ.

3. *Repent now.* Cut off all contact with the other woman, leaving no threads of contact that can lead back into a sinful relationship with her. It may be tempting today or tomorrow to recontact the other woman "just to make sure she's okay." It may be good for *someone* to check on her, *but it shouldn't be you.* Remember that he who renounces his sin finds mercy (Proverbs 28:13).

4. *Humble yourself before your wife.* After confessing your sin against her, explicitly ask her forgiveness. Don't soften your confession with anemic phrasing such as this: "Look, I'm sorry. Things were bad in our marriage, and I just felt a need to look for some personal happiness." That's not a true confession of sin. That's not humble enough.

Better to say something like this: "Honey, I am so sorry. I have sinned against God and against you. I broke my wedding vows to you. I sinned by becoming involved with another woman. I'm so sorry for how I've hurt you deeply and betrayed your trust. I understand if you need time to process all this and pray about your response. When you are ready, I would be so humbled if you would forgive me. I am willing to work on our marriage. I want to do what it takes to prove I've repented, and I don't ever want to do anything like this again. I am planning to get some counseling and to set up some personal accountability. I would be grateful if you would join me in the counseling sessions."

Restoring your wife's trust, regaining her heart, may take time—maybe lots of time. Don't demand quick words of forgiveness so you can get on with feeling good about yourself again. It doesn't always work out that way. But thanks to God, marriages have been saved after experiencing the crushing pain of adultery.

If you know a couple whose marriage has been restored and is still intact and growing years later, ask them if they would mentor you and your wife through your own restoration process.

Resisting the Bait in the First Place

How can those who have *not* fallen into the sin of adultery avoid taking that tempting but terrifying hook? How can we avoid the sin of adultery?

1. *Confess your own vulnerability.* Steve Farrar reminds us, "Better men than us have gone down. None of us are exempt. We are in spiritual warfare and given the wrong circumstances, any one of us could go down at any time."[5]

We must heed the warning of 1 Corinthians 10:12, "If you think you are standing firm, be careful that you don't fall!"

A few years ago when a dear sister in Christ in our church was caught in adultery, I found myself thinking, *I can't believe she did that!* But the Spirit impressed me almost immediately with the question, "What does that reaction say about your view of yourself, Larry? That you would never fall into such a sin?" Humbled, I realized I should have grieved over her sin and then prayed, "Lord, that could well have been me. I am no better than she. Oh, God, I so desperately need your protective grace in my life each day, each hour, each moment."

2. *When faced with temptation, always look for the way out.* On the heels of Paul's warning to the Corinthians about the dangers of self-assurance, he reminds us, "No temptation has seized you except what is common to man. And God is faithful; he will not let you be tempted beyond what you can bear. But when you are tempted, he will also provide a way out so that you can stand up under it" (1 Corinthians 10:13).

Sometimes the "way out" is not to get ourselves into compromising situations in the first place. For example, through our kids' courtship years, our family had an inflexible "three-person rule." They were not permitted to be alone in a private place with their sweethearts—not our home, not an apartment, not a parked car. There always had to be a third person around—a parent, a sibling, a roommate. Why would we married men give ourselves a lower standard?

During many years of pastoral ministry, I have refused to meet with a woman alone. Although some might consider this an antiquated standard, if a single woman, or a wife whose husband refuses to come, asks me for counseling, I require that she bring a trusted friend. If she cannot find someone to bring, I have asked my wife to join us. If the female counselee can't agree to that, I explain that I cannot serve her as a counselor. I will try to find a godly older woman to meet with her, but I cannot meet her alone. This creates some awkward situations, but I must always remember that I am not above temptation. Why foolishly put myself in a compromising situation?

This policy has also encouraged my wife over the years, assuring her that my heart is for her and her alone.

3. *Face the cost of committing the sin of adultery.* Solomon wisely taught his son the danger signs and the costs of sexual sin. Those of us with sons should do the same. A so-called affair with another woman might look enticing, but looks are deceptive. Solomon writes, "The lips of an adulteress drip honey, and her speech is smoother than oil; but in the end she is bitter as gall, sharp as a double-edged sword. Her feet go down to death; her steps lead straight to the grave" (Proverbs 5:3-5). Here are a few of the most common costs of taking the bait of sexual temptation:

- Adultery leads to profound disappointment. What looked so good at first ends up being an illusion. Steve Farrar writes, "The lure of adultery is that the other woman will truly meet your needs. The lie of adultery is that no other human on the face of the earth, no matter how alluring, interesting, or beautiful, has the capacity to fully meet the needs of another human being.

That's why adultery is the ultimate hoax. *It promises what it cannot deliver.*"[6]

- Adultery leads to financial ruin. Solomon writes, "Keep to a path far from [an adulteress]... lest strangers feast on your wealth and your toil enrich *another man's house*"— (Proverbs 5:8,10, emphasis added). That other man may be your wife's attorney!

- Adultery ruins reputations and families. Solomon warns that the adulterer will ultimately say, "I have come to the brink of utter ruin in the midst of the whole assembly (Proverbs 5:14). Consider the costs to your children as well.

- Most important of all, God, Himself, sees the sin of adultery—even that adultery you think you can keep secret. And it offends Him greatly. "A man's ways are in full view of the LORD," Solomon writes, "and he examines all his paths" (Proverbs 5:21).[7]

The Best Defense: A Good Offense

Paul's words to the Corinthian church are helpful here: "Flee from sexual immorality. All other sins a man commits are outside his body, but he who sins sexually sins against his own body. Do you not know that your body is a temple of the Holy Spirit, who is in you, whom you have received from God? *You are not your own; you were bought at a price. Therefore honor God with your body*" (1 Corinthians 6:18-20, emphasis added).

The best defense against the sin of adultery is a good offense. Right in the middle of Solomon's warning to his son about the dangers of adultery he gives this explicit counsel: "Drink water from your own cistern, running water from your own well. ...May your fountain be blessed, and may you rejoice in the wife of your youth. A loving doe, a graceful deer—may her breasts satisfy you always, may you ever be captivated by her love" (Proverbs 5:15, 18–20).

Investing in your marriage, cultivating your love for your wife, and enjoying the God-given blessing of marital intimacy are wonderful hedges against adultery. In *Learning from the Sages,* Bible commentator Kenneth T. Aitken explained it this way: "Here we have a passage which speaks enthusiastically about the joys and delights of the sexual relations between husband and wife. Enjoyment, not procreation, is its theme. This theme is taken up in the Song of Solomon, that lovely celebration of human love and fidelity between bride and bridegroom."[8]

Our passionate love for our wives, expressed in joyful sexual relations, makes any adulterous relationship a cheap counterfeit. As a dear older woman once said, "If your shoes are under your own bed, they won't be under the bed of some other woman." Does your wife know that your heart is for her and her alone?

Maybe there isn't and never has been another woman in your life. Praise God! But might there be other mistresses? Do you speak with more passion about or devote more of your heart to your job or your ministry or your hobby than you do to "the wife of your youth?" Might your wife feel she's getting your leftover attention and affection? Are you giving her the message, "I gave at the office"? Might she feel that your ministry or your hobby or your prized possession has become a mistress, competing for the affection you have promised her?

Some wives feel that their husbands have yet to cut the apron strings, still preferring the attention and approval of Mom or Dad to hers. In Bill McCartney's book, *What Makes a Man?*, authors Gary Smalley and John Trent write a chapter entitled, "The Promises You Make to Your Wife." In it they give important biblical counsel in this regard: "There is a verse used in almost all wedding ceremonies that usually gets as much attention as a distant relative standing in the reception line. Yet within one sentence is a key to successful relationships…"For this reason a man shall 'leave' father and mother and 'cleave' to his wife."[9]

While we can and should honor our parents and even seek their counsel as a younger married couple, our wives should never feel they are on the losing side of some competition for our love and loyalty.

Christ calls you and me to love our wives with a peerless love. Derek Prince says, "She should always have the confidence that to her husband she is the most important person in the world."[10]

DISCUSSION QUESTIONS AND ACTION STEPS
A Peerless Love (Part 2)

Discussion Questions

1. When we give in to various temptations that compromise our peerless love for our wives, we often try to justify ourselves in our minds or even to our wives. Read 1 Corinthians 10:12–13. How does this passage address our tendency to excuse ourselves for yielding to temptation?

2. What are some warning signs that might indicate you are letting your heart wander away from your commitment to a peerless love for your wife?

3. Why do you think is it so difficult for Christian men to discuss the lure of temptation and to confess their sins to one another—especially in the sexual realm?

4. How might your church be more intentional in strengthening men to resist the temptations of lust and adultery? How might the men in your church more faithfully minister to one another in this important area of life?

Action Steps

1. What might your wife consider competition for your affections? Your job? Sports? TV? Time on the computer? A hobby? Without defending yourself, ask her.

2. Talk with your accountability partners about how you will humbly but firmly intervene in one another's lives if you see signs that someone has compromised his peerless love for his wife. What will that intervention look like? Read Galatians 6:1, and then discuss your commitment to watch out for one another.

3. Talk to your wife this week about your desire to be a one-woman-man, devoted to her in all areas of your life. Humbly ask for her prayer support and invite her to confront you if she sees or feels that you have compromised that commitment. Take some time and pray together about it.

5

A Practical Love

Our kids are all grown and married now. However, when they were growing up, I tried to teach them important life lessons. Some grew out of our systematic studies during family devotions. Others arose spontaneously as we encountered various people and situations together in our daily family life. Some lessons were rather lighthearted, such as "Books are our friends!" More sobering ones gave our kids important guidelines for living wisely in this fallen world.

One of the more solemn and memorable life maxims I recall (I hope they do, too) was this: "If someone tells you one thing with his lips and a different thing with his life, believe his life. He's lying with his lips."

What was my point? I was warning our children that hypocrites will try to mislead them with their words though their lives will reveal something very different. It's a sad but important lesson in navigating the troubled waters of our culture. None of us wants to think of himself as a hypocrite, yet I suppose everyone who has ever walked on this planet has been hypocritical to some degree—except One.

Jesus Christ, The Consistent Lover

Jesus is the only Man whose life perfectly corresponded with the words of His lips. There was never any inconsistency. He was entirely free from hypocrisy. What Jesus said and how Jesus lived matched—every time.

Let's take as our prime example Jesus' love for His church. He told His people He loved them. In the upper room on the night before His crucifixion, Jesus looked at His disciples and assured them, "As the Father has loved me, so have I loved you. Now remain in my love." Then He continued, "My command is this: Love each other as I have loved you" (John 15:9 and 12). With His lips Jesus assured us of His love, but did His life back up His words? Did He do more than *say* He loved His people? We can think of a variety of ways Jesus put His words of love into action. The very fact that He came to this earth demonstrated His love. He voluntarily left the glories and comforts of a sinless heaven to come in human form to this sin-filled, curse-infected world. While on this earth, He showed loving compassion to those suffering from sickness, bereavement, and sin.

The focal point of His love, though, is the cross. Immediately after commissioning His followers to love each other as He loved them, He explained, "Greater love has no one than this, that he lay down his life for his friends" (John 15:13). Hours later that is exactly what Jesus did. He voluntarily laid down His own life in order to redeem His much-loved church: "Christ loved the church and gave himself up for her" (Ephesians 5:25). Jesus' life matched His lips—perfectly.

How can we mirror that kind of consistent love to our wives?

Becoming Our Wives' Practical Lover

Do those two words—*practical lover*—sound like they belong to-gether? Usually when we hear the word *lover* our thoughts turn to passion, romance, and sex. Those things are part of being a great lover to your wife, and we'll talk about those aspects of love later in chapter 9, "A Passionate Love." So hang in there! (If you're tempted to turn to that chapter now, don't forget to come back to these thoughts here on Practical Love!)

In this context, the following definition of the word *practical* may fit best: "Concerned with practice or use rather than theory; inclined to action rather than speculation."[1] In other words, husbands who are practical lovers do more than *say* words of love to their wives; they put their love into action.

In our quest to be like Christ in our love for our wives, how can we mirror Him in obeying the command of Ephesians 5:25: "Husbands, love your wives, just as Christ loved the church *and gave himself up for her*"? (emphasis added).

We want to continue to assure our wives of our love by saying with our lips "I love you." Jesus was never tight-lipped in expressing His love for His people. On the night before the cross He reassured His followers, "As the Father has loved me, so have I loved you" (John 15:9).

You may have heard the well-worn story of the old farmer and his wife who went in for marriage counseling. The wife complained that her husband never said those all-important words, "I love you." His brusque self defense? "I told you on our wedding day, 'I love you,' and if I ever change my mind, I'll let you know!"

We smile and shake our heads at this absurd story. But in all honesty, how often do *we* reassure our wives that we love them? Wouldn't our wives appreciate hearing us say those three little words more often?

After all these years of married life, it seems my wife never tires of my *saying* those power-packed words. In the morning she enjoys my waking her with a kiss, followed by "I love you, Gladine" and a few moments of snuggling. Before heading off for a busy day, it's another kiss and another reminder, "I love you." Arriving home in the evening gives me another opportunity for a smooch and another "I love you." And as I turn off the light by the bed each night, it's another kiss and another "I love you."

But those words must not be *merely* words. Our lives must match our lips. The apostle John explained, "This is how we know what love is: Jesus Christ laid down his life for us. And we ought to lay down our lives for our brothers [*and our wives!*]" (addition mine). "Dear children, let us not love with words or tongue but with actions and in truth" (1 John 3:16 and 18).

Imagine applying those words from 1 John 3 in the context of our marriages. The love we have for our wives must go beyond our words. It must be expressed with actions and in truth. In the words of Dr. Lloyd-Jones, "Love is not something merely talked about; love is not just something to be written about [in poems or songs]. Love is the most practical thing in the world. For it is not what you and

I say that finally proves whether we are truly manifesting love; it is what we do."[2]

So, how do we demonstrate Christlike "practical" love?

Serving Our Wives with Practical Love

It's easy in our culture to think that our wives exist to serve us, never considering that to model Christ *we* must learn to serve *them*. Remembering that we are the heads of our homes, we may tend to assume that the words *leader* and *servant* are somehow incompatible. Let's take a fresh gaze at the Perfect Lover.

During that same evening in the upper room, on the night before the cross, we see Jesus welding together the roles of leader and servant. The Passover meal had already begun, yet no one had volunteered to do the lowly, customary task of washing the others' feet. Astonishingly, it was not Peter, John, or Andrew who rose to do that menial task. It was the Leader. It was Jesus Himself. In *Walking Like Jesus Did*, I write about this awkward event.

> John records this bit of fascinating background before he tells the story of the Master washing the feet of His disciples: "Jesus knew that the Father had put all things under his power, and that he had come from God and was returning to God" (John 13:3)...
>
> What was John's point? Jesus was not operating out of a position of weakness, but of power, not out of a position of insecurity, but of certainty. He was secure in His relationship with His heavenly Father. He was confident in His impending return to His place of honor and glory. He was very much aware, also, that the Father had put all things "under His power," or more literally, "into His hands."
>
> So, very much aware of His powerful ability and authority, what did Jesus do? Rather than demanding to *be* served by His followers, Jesus voluntarily chose to serve them! He chose to use His power and authority to serve His men by doing the most menial of jobs —even though His men had been displaying a disturbing pride in their debate and lack of initiative in serving one another.[3]

Our Perfect Model shows us how to use our positions as heads of the home not to be served but to serve. When you say, "I love you" to your wife, does she smile with that knowing look that says, "Yes, I know you do. I see it in how you serve me here in our home"?

In what practical ways do we mirror Christ who "loved the church and gave himself up for her"?

The Practical Love of Load Sharing

Many of us husbands have a preconceived notion of which household chores are "manly." You know, things like mowing the grass, trimming the hedges, cleaning the gutters, and changing the batteries in the smoke detectors. Usually men are okay with such tasks. But somehow we might ignore our wives as they struggle to carry the laundry to the washing machine, or we may walk away from the dinner table without helping to clear the dirty dishes. In some traditions, those tasks are considered "woman's work."

But I wonder how many wives would feel truly loved if we husbands would jump up from watching the game on TV and say, "Here, honey, let me carry that." How many wives would be astonished to hear their husbands say, "Honey, you've had a big day. Why don't you go sit in the recliner and read for a little while? The kids and I will clean up after dinner."

Why is it that a husband can be in the same room as a crying baby and shout to his wife at the other end of the house, "Honey, the baby's crying! I think maybe his diaper needs to be changed!"

Men, let's serve our wives with practical love. Let's take the initiative to change the diaper, to do the dishes, to take out the trash, to run the kids to practice.

We can paraphrase Philippians 2:3–5 to apply specifically to our relationships to our wives: "Do nothing out of selfish ambition or vain conceit, but in humility consider your wives better than yourselves. Each of you husbands should look not only to your own interests, but also to the interests of your wife. Your attitude should be the same as that of Christ Jesus."

Love is that practical! It's considering our wives more important than ourselves, and then, with the attitude of Christ, serving our wives in humility.

Here's a challenging assignment: Ask your wife what would make her feel loved. Her answer may surprise you. Many women just want their husbands to show they care by taking more initiative in carrying the load at home.

The Practical Love of Active Listening

Another way some wives would feel more loved is if their husbands simply took time to talk with them and listen to them—really listen to them. Why not back up your words of affection with the practical love of making time to sit and tenderly converse with your wife?

For years I was callous to my wife's longing for me to listen regularly and attentively to her heart. I tend to be a goal-oriented person with lots on my daily to-do list. I've somehow thought it virtuous always to be multitasking, so I naively assumed I could be working on some other project while listening to Gladine. I could do tasks in the kitchen or skim through the mail while she told me about her day.

Then one day in frustration she cried out, "I can't see you listening to me!"

At first I chuckled, thinking her comment humorous—even cute. But eventually her appeal began to sink in to my too-busy mind. She really did want to "see me listening" to her. She longed for me to demonstrate, practically, my love for her by laying aside all other preoccupations—no mail, no laptop, no TV, no newspaper, no cell phone. She wanted my face turned toward hers, my eyes meeting hers, and my mind engaged in actively listening not only to her words but also to her heart from which her words were flowing.

Jim George writes, "Listening is an act of love. When you are listening, you are saying, 'I value you as my wife and I want to hear what you have to say.'"[4]

This practical demonstration of love does not mean passively sitting nearby while your wife talks "at" you and you contribute an obligatory—though absentminded—"Uh-huh" now and then.

Listening as a demonstration of practical love is a very *active* exercise, or should we say *interactive*? Our tendency as men is to give our wives a quick "listen," then attempt some just-as-quick fix to whatever concern she just expressed so we can get on to other things (or back to the TV or newspaper).

Guys, our wives don't want us to fix them. They want us to care—to care not only about the issue at hand but also about them and how this issue might be affecting them. I confess I'm still learning how to demonstrate this kind of love. And I'm finding out that we often need to sit on our tongues for a while and not interrupt with some insensitive remark such as, "Oh, it's not that bad," or "Yeah, I know how you feel."

In *Marriage in the Whirlwind* Bill and Pam Farrel write, "Often, a wife will try to tell her husband how she is *feeling* and he responds by telling her what she should be *doing*. Those are not necessarily the same thing."[5]

Instead of presuming, why don't we ask, "Honey, how do you feel about that issue?" Or maybe we can engage her with, "You seem to be very concerned about that. Can you help me understand better what you're feeling? I'd really like to know what's on your heart." Even if we discern that our wife's response to a situation may not be what God would desire from her, demonstrating a loving concern for her heart first will open doors for us to later gently lead her on in grace to a godly response.

One of the best things for our marriage in recent years has been carving out time each day to talk together as husband and wife. Walking together for exercise for 30 to 40 minutes most mornings has not only provided some semblance of physical fitness but also has been a great boost for the health of our marriage. We are almost never interrupted while we walk early in the morning through our neighborhood streets. We can talk—and listen—to each other. We also try to eat breakfast together most mornings, lingering awhile to read from the Bible together, to talk about its application, and to pray as husband and wife. Usually, we also make time at dinner or later in the evening to listen to the events of each other's day. It's love that's so *practical*.

You who still have children at home may have to work harder at carving out that time than those of us who are empty nesters. You might have to get up before the children and have an early morning cup of coffee or tea together. You might have to be more diligent in making sure the kids have a fixed bedtime so you and your wife can have some evening minutes together. But please make the time to exhibit this practical demonstration of how much you love your wife. She will bless you for it.

DISCUSSION QUESTIONS AND ACTION STEPS
A Practical Love

Discussion Questions

1. Read Philippians 2:3–5 together as a group. Then discuss ways in which this principle could transform your marriage.

2. What are the household chores that you, the husband, generally do in your home? What are the chores your wife generally does? How did you come to that plan? Are you and your wife both content with it? Have you asked her?

3. Is there some task your wife has wanted you to do for some time, but you keep procrastinating? What's keeping you from doing it?

4. Tell the guys in your group a story of a time you surprised your wife by doing something unexpected that really seemed to please her. (If you can't think of anything, it's OK to surprise her with something this week!)

5. Read John 13:1–17 as a group. What might be some ways you as husbands could "wash the feet" of your wives?

Action Steps

1. During this next week, look for three ways or times each day to come right out and say, "I love you" to your wife. At least one of these three should be a new daily pattern of expressing your love. For example, say, "I love you" every day as you go off to work or every evening as you say good night. Find some other creative ways of verbally telling your wife that she is precious to you. For example, take a few moments to call her or e-mail her or text her during the day "just to say 'I love you!'"

2. Pick an evening during the next week, and after dinner encourage your wife to sit in her favorite chair with her favorite

reading material while you (and the kids?) clean up the kitchen and put everything away.

3. If you do not already do so, pick a time that will work each day for you to focus on listening to your wife's heart. Make it a habit to lay down all unnecessary distractions (no TV, no newspaper in hand, no text messaging) and really listen to her, asking her questions not only about the facts of her day, but also about her feelings. Even if it feels awkward at first, keep trying! Next time your group gets together, tell the others how it went.

6

A Protecting Love

I honestly don't remember what I said. I guess that's not what matters now. The painfully beneficial lesson that followed is what counts. That's what I remember. I was 16, proud, and rude. My mother had obviously given me some parental directive, and I was too full of myself to receive it. More concerned about my own agenda and priorities, I had sassed her—undeniably a sin. I'm grateful the details have slipped my memory, and I hope my elderly mother has forgotten them as well! And I'm grateful for the astonishing grace of God. The encounter that followed—a somber meeting with my Dad—has stuck in my soul for nearly 40 years.

This was no angry, "Stop it!" from my truck driver dad. He set me down at the kitchen table, and with an uncharacteristically quavering voice and moist eyes, he gave me this unforgettable charge: "I don't ever want to hear you talk to my wife that way again!" His words seemed so resolute, so determinedly passionate.

Though I was only 16, and years away from my own marriage to Gladine, Dad taught me an important lesson about a husband's love for his wife. He hadn't planned a father-son lesson about husbanding that day. He simply modeled the way a Christlike husband must love his wife with a protective love.

I can still recall his words clearly. He had not said, "I don't ever want to hear you talk to your mother that way again." No, he chose different words: "I don't ever want to hear you talk to *my wife* that way again!" The words that grabbed my mind and heart that day in the kitchen were the words *my wife*. He was speaking not merely as my father at that moment, but as the loving, devoted husband of my mother. He was loving her by protecting her—from me, a brash, back-talking teen-aged son.

Jesus' Loving Protection of His Bride

Jesus does such a good job of protecting us as His church that we rarely give it much thought. He is not an uninvolved or insensitive husband. As our Savior, He is constantly caring for us and protecting us moment by moment. "He is able to save completely those who come to God through him, because he always lives to intercede for them" (Hebrews 7:25). Lou Priolo writes, "The Greek verb from which the word 'savior' is derived…involves keeping someone safe and sound, rescuing him/her from danger or destruction, saving that person from judgment, evil or injury; peril, disease or death."[1]

Jesus protects us from Satan and from the penalty of our own sin. This cost Him His life, freely offered on the cross to protect us from the devouring predator, the Devil, as well as from the damning consequences of our sinfulness.

Our Shepherd's Protection

Using the analogy of a shepherd with his flock, Jesus assures us, "I am the good shepherd. The good shepherd lays down his life for the sheep. The hired hand is not the shepherd who owns the sheep. So when he sees the wolf coming, he abandons the sheep and runs away. Then the wolf attacks the flock and scatters it. The man runs away because he is a hired hand and cares nothing for the sheep" (John 10:11–13). Jesus never shirked His commitment to protect us, though His love cost Him dearly.

In the graphic words of Puritan Thomas Watson, "He leaped into the sea of his Father's wrath to save his spouse from drowning."[2] Indeed, His loving protection extends beyond that glorious yet horrifying day at Calvary. Paul tells us the protecting love of Jesus is ongoing: "The Lord is faithful, and he will strengthen and protect you from the evil one" (2 Thessalonians 3:3).

The Holy Spirit's Protection

Jesus continues to show his loving protection of us, His bride, by giving us His Holy Spirit. Hours before the cross, Jesus comforted His anxious, confused disciples by promising, "I will ask the Father, and he will give you another Counselor to be with you forever—the Spirit of truth" (John 14:16–17). This promised Counselor is our divine helper, defender, and protector against the attacks of our accuser and his demonic and human cohorts.

Our Church Leaders' Protection

Have you ever thought about the elders in your church being an evidence of Jesus' incessant protecting love for you? Jesus Christ gave these men to the church (Ephesians 4:11) and charged them with the responsibility of protecting the body from destructive forces—both internal and external (Acts 20:28–31; Hebrews 13:17). Oh, how Jesus loves us, His bride! He provides the protection we need now and for eternity. How comforting to rest in His loving protection. Paul writes, "May your whole spirit, soul and body be kept blameless at the coming of our Lord Jesus Christ. The one who calls you is faithful and he will do it" (1 Thessalonians 5:23–24).

Our Loving Protection of Our Wives

Does your wife feel your protecting love? Why not ask her? Let's think through some practical ways to mirror, in our own marriages, the love Christ has for His bride.

Protecting Her Physically

Physical care is probably what most men think of when challenged to protect their wives. Christian radio host Dennis Rainey quips, "Imagine lying in bed late at night and hearing a noise downstairs. What husband would, in good conscience, nudge his wife and say, 'I'm scared. You go'?"[3] It seems the Lord built into husbands a willingness to demonstrate love to their wives (and to demonstrate their own manliness) by protecting their wives physically. If the husband is at all available, he will almost always be the one who checks on that "bump in the night," squashes the spider, or disposes of the dead mouse dragged in by the family cat. While not as exciting as warding off lions, tigers, and bears, here are more ways we can assure our wives of our love through physical protection:

- *Make your home safe.* Why not make it a habit to secure the house before retiring to bed? Let your wife know that you will check the doors, making sure they are locked and that any security system you might have is activated.

- *Keep chivalry alive:* Walk on the street side of the sidewalk, open doors for her, turn on the lights in a dark house before she enters.

- *Take care of your wife's car.* Does the car need gas? Fill it up for her. If you live in a northern climate, give yourself some extra minutes in the morning to clear the ice and snow from her car's windows. How about warming up that icy vehicle before she leaves for work or runs errands? Even if you aren't a mechanic, demonstrate your love for your wife by monitoring car maintenance schedules and making sure any necessary repair work is done as soon as possible.

- *Help her take care of her personal health.* Often it is the wife who must intervene in her husband's health, but occasionally a husband needs to take initiative in protecting his wife's health. This may take an extra dose of sensitivity to avoid demeaning her in any way. Is she getting enough rest? What can you, as a loving husband, do to make sure she gets the rest she needs? Does she work full time while also trying to run the home nearly single-handedly? Could your family get by on one income—or even one-and-a-half incomes? Could *you* do more to help around the house? If you are not currently "domesticated," why not humbly ask your wife to teach you how to do the laundry or housecleaning? Could she teach you some basic cooking skills so she is not left to do all the kitchen work herself? Could you demonstrate love for your weary wife by working with your children on their homework or doing their assigned chores, relieving your wife of some of the many tasks on her list? Let her know you care about her health, and then back it up with action.

- *Set an example in health matters.* Do you need to take more loving initiative in setting an example in healthful eating habits? Finally breaking that tobacco habit? Beginning an exercise program with her? Making sure she gets her annual physical? You can demonstrate protective love for your wife by promoting healthful life habits in your family. A loving husband takes initiative in caring for his wife in these often-neglected ways.

Though the days of sweeping the love of your life off her feet and onto your white charger are now relegated to movies, you can still demonstrate your protective love by doing such thoughtful things as these.

Protecting Her Emotionally

Now it gets a little tougher. The idea of demonstrating love by physically protecting our wives seems easy for most men to grasp. It's concrete. It's manly. However, most husbands struggle to understand their wives' emotions. If you don't understand her emotionally, how are you supposed to demonstrate your love by protecting her in this elusive realm of everyday life?

Why not ask her? This will stretch us, guys, but just asking the question itself will probably be a huge demonstration of our love for our wives. Here are some ideas my wife has given me along with a few ideas I've picked up doing marriage counseling over the years:

- *Protect her from the stress of overworking.* We can demonstrate Christlike love by protecting our wives from unnecessarily feeling overwhelmed. Some wives—like some husbands—are overachievers, trying to cram 25 (or more) hours of activities into a 24-hour day. My wife, Gladine, appreciates my sitting down with her at least weekly to talk through all the various things we feel we "need" to do. She doesn't want me playing the military general, telling her, "I want you to do this and this, but not that and that," but she does appreciate my showing a true interest in her upcoming week and helping her think through priorities. Sometimes it's helpful to suggest lovingly, "Why don't you focus on such-and-such this week? We can let some of those other things wait for a less busy time." Gladine especially likes me to stop and say, "Let's seek the Lord's guidance on this before we go further." She says praying together, talking together, and planning together makes her feel loved and protected.

- *Protect her from unnecessary worries regarding the financial well being of your family.* Sometimes we men can be defensive when our wives verbalize their worries about finances. We think they're attacking our ability to earn an adequate income. But a more helpful response is a humble, God-centered attitude, holding our wife's hand and together going to the throne of the King to seek His wisdom and provision. The antidote to financial worries is not necessarily getting more money (though some husbands may need to consider a job change in order to provide better for their families). Taking initiative in budgeting the money you do have can assure your wife that you really do care about the family's financial welfare. Why not develop the habit of using part of New Year's Day to work on an annual budget together? Then keep tabs now and then on the progress. Working on this together can reassure your wife and relieve her from the stress of not knowing where the money will come from or where it is going.

- *Protect her from the emotional strain of harmful people.* Husbands need to be aware of people in their precious wives' lives who can do them great emotional harm. Remember what my dad told me in the situation I related at the beginning of this chapter? Apparently he is not the only husband who demonstrated love to his wife by protecting her from a sassy teenager. Steve Farrar tells a similar story of a man who protected his wife by correcting his disrespectful teenage son. The wife's response to her husband's loving but firm defense?

> In all of our years of marriage you have done some wonderful things for me. You have given me wonderful gifts

and we have taken some very special trips. But nothing you have ever done for me has meant more to me than the way that you demanded that our son respect me. You will never know how much that let me know how much you love me and value me.[4]

Would your wife say the same about you? Do you need to make some changes in how you protect your wife from the harmful treatment of others—even your own children?

- *Protect her from sexual temptation.* Yet another way we can protect our wives emotionally is to provide satisfying intimacy in marriage. We'll discuss this more fully in the chapter, "A Passionate Love," but we must also consider it here. Wives who feel neglected by their husbands—romantically and sexually—are at a greater risk when another man pays special attention to them. Men, protect your wife from unnecessary temptation by loving them romantically and sexually, providing joy and satisfaction in the intimacy of your marriage.

Protecting Her Spiritually

If the previous section on protecting our wives emotionally is a stretch, this area of loving protection is uncharted waters for most husbands. How are we to protect our wives *spiritually*? What does that look like?

Our wives, like us, are faced with various temptations—both internal and external. How does the old hymn say it? "Just as I am, tho' tossed about with many a conflict, many a doubt, fightings and fears within, without"?[5]

What is our role as husbands in demonstrating Christlike love by protecting our wives spiritually?

First, remember that an ounce of prevention is worth a pound of cure. Or, to put it another way, "If you regularly water the grass you won't have to spend as much time putting out brush fires."

Second, *make time* to nourish your wife spiritually:

- Pray with her.
- Read the Bible and other solid Christian books with her.

- Block out devotional time with her.

- Talk to her in everyday conversations about Christ and about His promises of grace.

- Listen to Christian music that builds her up spiritually.

- Get involved in your local church and a small group, where both you and your wife can develop a noticeable depth in your enjoyment of Christ and your likeness to Him. If your church doesn't teach and live out God's Word, find one that does. Make sure both you and your wife are getting the spiritual nutrition you need.

Third, study your wife's heart. This is the key to these spiritually healthy, everyday life habits.

- What temptations does she face most often? Do you know? Do you need to ask? Is she tempted to anger and bitterness? To fantasy and lust? To discontent and grumbling? To unbelief and despair?

- How can you help her resist these temptations? Are there specific ways you should be praying with her? Are there Scriptures on these subjects you can lovingly suggest studying together?

- Don't leave her alone in battling these temptations if you can come alongside her to help protect her.

The first husband who ever lived (whom theologians also call the first Adam) should have protected his wife, Eve, when the serpent hissed his seductive temptations. After all, Adam was right there "with her" (Genesis 3:6). Jesus Christ (whom theologians call the second Adam), models a husband's proper response to spiritual attack. He never abdicates His responsibility to protect His bride, the church (2 Thessalonians 3:3). Looking to Him—His example, His strength, His grace—let's love our wives with a protecting love.

DISCUSSION QUESTIONS AND ACTION STEPS
A Protecting Love

Discussion Questions

1. What are some protecting ways that Jesus demonstrates His love for us, His bride? What is He protecting us from?

2. Can you recall an incident in which you took the initiative to protect your wife from potential physical, emotional, or spiritual harm? As a husband, how did demonstrating love to your wife that way make you feel?

3. The apostle Peter tells us to treat our wives with respect (1 Peter 3:7). A literal translation would be "grant them honor." But our culture often degrades women. What are some ways we can swim against the current and protect our wives physically, emotionally, and spiritually?

Action Steps

1. During your prayer time this week, thank the Lord for demonstrating His love by protecting you from the Evil One (2 Thessalonians 3:3). Thank Him also for leaders in your church who faithfully seek to protect your church from spiritual harm. (See Acts 20:28.)

2. Sometime this week ask your wife this question: How can I better show my love for you by protecting you? Give her time to think about it if necessary. Especially explore ways you could take initiative in protecting her emotionally and spiritually.

3. If your wife expresses feelings of being overwhelmed, take time to tenderly ask questions so that you can better understand what's happening in her life and how that's affecting her physically, emotionally, and spiritually. Resist the temptation to suggest a "quick fix." Instead, express compassion, and then pray with her, asking the Lord's direction and strength. *After you have done that,* begin to discuss with her some possible solutions toward which the Lord may be directing you.

7

A Purposeful Love

It's time again—time to work on the next five-year plan. I have had the privilege of serving our church as senior pastor for more than 26 years. Over the years our church has continued to grow, and with that growth has come the need to evaluate and plan regularly. Are we on track with God's revealed will for us as a church? Are we being sensitive to ways He wants us to change and minister in the future? Every five years the church's leadership spends lots of time praying, evaluating, and planning, laying out a plan for the *next* five years—all submitted to His sovereign will, of course. It's time again to lay out the next five-year plan.

You who are in business, academia, and parachurch ministries know what I'm talking about. Some of you are good at it. It gets your creative juices flowing to prayerfully envision your business or your ministry five years in the future and lay out a plan to pursue that destination as God providentially leads and enables.

However, as Bob Lepine notes, "Many of those same business-men, who can establish a successful plan for a company, are clue-less when it comes time to think strategically about the spiritual, emotional, physical and social needs of their wives. Ask them about their five-year plan for their marriage, and you're likely to get a 'deer-in-the-headlights' look."[1]

A five-year plan for my marriage? Who ever heard of such a thing? Maybe the idea sounds odd for a couple of reasons.

First, few of us think about our marriages as having goals. We might have career goals or retirement goals, but that's about it. Any marriage goals we set usually center on finances. My hunch is that very few husbands have prayerfully thought about spiritual goals for their marriages.

Second, few husbands have given serious thought to *their* roles in leading their wives toward specific spiritual goals. We may ask, "Is my wife's spiritual development really my responsibility?"

Here's an interesting exercise: Look at yourself in the mirror and ask, "What do I believe God wants my wife to be like at the end of our lives together, and what does He want me to do about helping her get there?" Better not try that too early in the morning—at least not until you've had your first cup of coffee. You're likely to get that "deer-in-the-headlights" look Lepine mentioned.

Mind blowing, isn't it? Yet by God's grace, this question should burn in the conscience of every husband who is following hard after Christ. "Lord, what do you want my wife to become, and what do you want me to do to help her get there?"

This concept is so new to most of us that we need some model—some prototype to look at if we are ever going to move forward in this dynamic love for our wives. Praise God, we do have a perfect Model! "Husbands, love your wives, just as Christ loved the church and gave himself up for her to make her holy, cleansing her by the washing with water through the word, *and to present her to himself as a radiant church, without stain or wrinkle or any other blemish, but holy and blameless.* In the same way husbands ought to love their wives" (Ephesians 5:25–28, emphasis added).

Jesus' Purposeful Love for His Bride

Jesus has plans for us, His bride—loving plans. To say it another way, He loves us with a *purposeful* love. While any consideration of Christ's love for His church must begin with Christ's saving work on the cross, it must not stop there. Dr. D. Martyn Lloyd-Jones once said, "He [Jesus Christ] cannot stop at the first step [justification]; he goes on to sanctify her. In other words, His death upon the Cross for us, and our sins, was simply the first step in this great process. And

He does not stop at the first step. He has a complete purpose for the church, and he will go through it all step by step."[2]

How far into the future do Jesus' plans for the church reach? One year? Five years? How about 10 years?

In Jesus' long-range love for His bride, He actually has His eyes on eternity. He is looking forward to that glorious Wedding Supper of the Lamb, when He returns to the earth for His bride. God allowed the elderly apostle John a glimpse into what is yet to come. This is John's account of that experience:

"I heard what sounded like a great multitude, like the roar of rushing waters and like loud peals of thunder, shouting: 'Hallelujah! For our Lord God Almighty reigns. Let us rejoice and be glad and give him glory! For the wedding of the Lamb has come, and his bride has made herself ready. Fine linen, bright and clean, was given her to wear. (Fine linen stands for the righteous acts of the saints.)" (Revelation 19:6–8).

That's why Paul says Jesus has set His eyes on "presenting" His bride to Himself as a "radiant church, without stain or wrinkle or any other blemish, but holy and blameless."[3] Jesus' love for us is not some mindless reaction to our love for Him. No. His love is very purposeful. He is leading us to a goal—a wondrous goal—of being His glorious bride on That Day.

What is that ultimate goal Jesus has for us, His bride? That we might reflect Him, be like Him. "Dear friends," John writes, "now we are children of God, and what we will be has not yet been made known. But we know that when he appears, we shall be *like him*, for we shall see him as he is" (1 John 3:2, emphasis added).

Jesus never loses sight of that ultimate goal for us. "He is not going to be satisfied until she is perfect. He wants to be able to present her to Himself a glorious church," writes Dr. Martyn Lloyd-Jones. Later, he illustrates it this way: "Think of the most beautiful bride you have ever seen. Multiply that by infinity, and still you do not begin to understand it. But that is what the church is going to be like."[4]

Our beauty as His bride—our "glory"—will be His glorious character seen in us. That has been His plan all along.

Everything the Lord brings into our lives—individually and as His bride—is for this ultimate purpose of transforming us to reflect His glory. It doesn't matter if the experiences are pleasurable or painful; they all serve God's ultimate purpose. "We know that in all things God works for the good of those who love him, who have been called according to his purpose. For those God foreknew *he also predestined to be conformed to the likeness of his Son*" (Romans 8:28–29, emphasis added). The Lord's love for us is always moving us toward that ultimate "good" of making us more like Christ. As Thomas Watson said many years ago, "Christ never thinks he has loved his spouse enough till he can see his own face in her."[5]

Preparing us for that glorious wedding day, He is leading us with purposeful love.

Our Purposeful Love for Our Wives

"In this same way, husbands ought to love their wives," Paul writes in Ephesians 5:28. As Christ loves with a purposeful love, so must we. Even as Christ has a wonderful goal for us as His bride and is leading us there, so we husbands are to have a God-honoring goal for our wives and lovingly lead them there "as long as we both shall live."

"What goal?" you ask. The idea of leading our wives toward an ultimate goal may still baffle us. It's tempting to pull the vehicle of our marriage into the gas station of worldly wisdom to get directions. But that doesn't work. Those directions will not help us get to the destination.

Sometimes in our stubborn pride we refuse to ask for directions from anybody. Left to ourselves, we tend to look inward, thinking we can come up with our own goals for our wives. Sadly, by default if not design, we may try to move our wives to become more like us! We foolishly think if our wives were just more like us, our marriages would sail more smoothly and our lives would be a lot more carefree.

On the contrary, why would God want us to make our wives into our own image? Our ultimate goal for our wives mirrors Jesus' ultimate goal for His bride—Christlikeness. "We, who with unveiled faces all reflect the Lord's glory, *are being transformed into his like-*

ness with ever-increasing glory, which comes from the Lord, who is the Spirit" (2 Corinthians 3:18, emphasis added). We husbands are primary tools in the hands of the Holy Spirit in that glorious process of molding our wives to become more and more like Christ. So it would be helpful to better understand how the Spirit uses us to serve our wives in this transformation process.

Our Example

The Holy Spirit uses the example of our everyday lives as husbands in shaping the character, priorities, and passions of our wives. What was the Apostle Paul's counsel to the people he was leading? "Follow my example, as I follow the example of Christ" (1 Corinthians 11:1). Isn't it sobering to picture ourselves saying those same words to our wives? Can you envision yourself saying with humble integrity these words: "Honey, the Lord has commissioned me, your husband, to help you become more like Jesus. So, watch my example, and follow me as I follow Christ"?

Serving our wives by giving them a real life example to follow obviously requires some understanding of what it means *for us* to follow Christ. The apostle John taught, "This is how we know we are in him: Whoever claims to live in him *must walk as Jesus did*" (1 John 2:5–6 emphasis added). Do you know how Jesus walked His life on this earth? It would be good for every husband concerned with purposefully loving his wife to make it a lifelong quest to know Christ in ever-increasing measure. As Christlike models for our precious wives, we need a practical understanding of His meekness, holiness, compassion, patience, forgiveness, joy, love, and more. We need to mirror those attributes of Christ in our own personal lives. Let's study Christ—not only for the sake of our own growth in sanctification,[6] but also for the spiritual growth of our wives.

Leading by everyday example can be a powerful influence. Author and pastor, John Piper says,

> Leadership is something you *are* as much as something you *do*. If you come out of your solitude with the aroma of Christ lingering in your life, your wife and children will sense intuitively that you are at the helm of the ship with

God's hand on your shoulder. Leadership techniques and strategies are all in vain if the man has not been with God. It's what we become in solitude with God that makes us spiritual leaders. If we fail here, we fail utterly.[7]

We might ask ourselves, "Is my wife more like Jesus today than she was on our wedding day because of the influence of my Christlike example?" Lord, please make it so! In the words of hymn writer Charles H. Gabriel, "More like the Master, I would ever be!"

Our Teaching

During our weekly breakfast together, one of the men in my accountability group unscrewed the cap of the restaurant saltshaker and also picked up a toothpick. With these props looking amusingly tiny in his large hands, he told us about a humbling but life-changing conversation he had with his wife. Although he had professed faith in Christ years before, he had never seriously devoted time and energy to growing in Christian maturity. In his own words, he had "never gotten off first base." He was struggling to live out his anemic faith in his business and in his home.

Then one day, his wife challenged him. She said he was trying to do battle in the world, but he'd never availed himself of the full armor of God. He had never been intentional about following the spiritual strategy of Ephesians 6:10–11: "Finally, be strong in the Lord and in his mighty power. Put on the full armor of God so that you can take your stand against the devil's schemes."

His wife gave him this visual illustration: Picking up the cap of a saltshaker, she counseled, "Your 'shield of faith' is the size of this salt shaker lid!" And holding up a toothpick she observed, "The 'sword of the Spirit,' you're using is the size of this toothpick!"

Ouch! The Lord used that wifely exhortation to get my friend's attention. There was a good explanation for his struggle to represent Christ in his business, his church, and his home. He had made little effort to grow in his own understanding and application of the Scriptures. With this new insight, he laid out a plan for daily Bible study and prayer. Over time he moved beyond first base, making observable strides in spiritual growth. His consistency in representing Christ at work and at home began to greatly improve—much to the encouragement of his wife.

Pastor John Piper challenged the men in the church he serves along these same lines. "To provide spiritual food for the family, you must know spiritual food. This means that a man must go hard after God. You can only lead spiritually if you are growing in your own knowledge of God and love for God. If you are feeding your soul with the Word of God, you will be drawn to feed your wife and your children."[8]

Steve Farrar gets even more specific when he writes, "Gentlemen, if we are going to be spiritual leaders for our wives and children…we need to make time to soak ourselves in God's Word; we need time to chew on what the Scripture is saying to us; we need time to come before God and ask Him to give us the wisdom we need to be His men in this world."[9]

We know if we want to be in shape physically, five minutes of exercise per day isn't going to cut it. Yet we somehow naively assume that five minutes of spiritual exercise will make us spiritually fit.

If we are going to be instruments in the hands of the Holy Spirit, serving our wives by teaching them the ways of God, we need to be much more serious about our own spiritual growth so we have something of spiritual substance to offer our wives. Bob Lepine says that we "must assume responsibility to nurture and disciple her. It's at the core of what it means to be a husband."[10]

How do we teach our wives? Lepine laments, "The truth is, for many Christian men, the idea of some formal time of Bible study or instruction is in their top ten list of threatening activities. We feel inadequate and unsure of ourselves."[11] Some men are intimidated at the idea, seeking to excuse themselves by saying "I don't have the gift of teaching." Yet teaching her might be as simple as setting aside some daily time to read a portion of Scripture with her, drawing attention to ways that passage is a comfort or a challenge to you. You may notice something in the day's reading that you think would be especially helpful to your wife as she faces challenges with which you can sympathize.

You don't have to have a library of commentaries at your disposal. I sometimes encourage men to find a good study Bible and to spend a few minutes reviewing the study helps before reading the passage with their wives. If you have not yet devoted any planned time of teaching your wife from the Scriptures, why not humbly ask the Lord's help today? Then pick a time, a place, and a passage, and get started. I suspect your wife will consider herself blessed to have a husband who loves her in such a spiritually purposeful way.

Our Encouragement

We can also purposefully love our wives by encouraging their Christlikeness through various spiritual growth opportunities. We touched on this in the previous chapter as it relates to spiritual protection, but we need to emphasize it here again with more ideas for purposefully leading our wives to the goal of Christlikeness:

Encourage spiritual growth opportunities outside the home. Facilitate her participation in spiritual learning opportunities—care groups, Sunday School classes, and sermons (maybe Dad needs to be the one to step out with the fussy child). Treat her to a seminar. Encourage her to read sound Christian books and magazines. Jim George advises, "Take an active role in assisting your wife's maturing process in the many facets of her life."[12] The very fact that you think about such opportunities for her growth and take the initiative in gently encouraging her to take advantage of them would surely refresh her soul and reassure her of your loving care.

Encourage spiritual growth opportunities in daily family life. As you go through everyday life, you may notice that your wife is feeling discouraged or even depressed. If you are like I am, you might feel hurt or even frustrated with her discouragement. It's so easy to feel as if her discouragement signals your failure somehow as a husband.

Many times I've wanted to "fix" my wife, either by lecturing her on her negative outlook or by trying to get her to find some silver lining to her clouded soul. Such reactions are shortsighted at best and selfish at worst. They are "godless." I'm leaving God out of the picture and doing little to serve my wife by drawing her to Christ, where she can find true joy. Gary Ricucci asks, "Do I constantly remind her of the gospel of grace and of God's active goodness on our behalf?"[13]

Men, if we are to serve our wives with a purposeful love that moves them steadily toward Christlikeness, we must be men of grace—men who revel in God's grace, speak of God's grace, model God's grace. "For the grace of God that brings salvation has appeared to all men. It teaches us to say 'No' to ungodliness and worldly passions, and to live self-controlled, upright and godly lives in this present age, while we wait for the blessed hope—the glorious appearing of our great God and Savior, Jesus Christ" (Titus 2:11–13).

The Main Point

At the time of this writing, my parents are looking forward to their 60th wedding anniversary.

Although I'm sure the years have flown by for them, that still seems like a long time to be married.

I've been reflecting on this thought: "If God allows both Gladine and me to live long lives, maybe we, too, will someday celebrate 60 years of marriage. If so, will I be able to look into her eyes on that day of celebration and know that, by God's grace, I have been a tool in the hand of the Holy Spirit, leading her to be more like Christ than she was on the day we became man and wife?"

This is my prayer: *May it be so, Lord! Please help me invest in my wife's soul. Help me, like You, to love my wife with a purposeful love, leading her step by step toward You.*

DISCUSSION QUESTIONS AND ACTION STEPS
A Purposeful Love

Discussion Questions

1. What is the Lord's goal for us? Toward what ultimate "good" is His love moving us? (See Romans 8:28–29 and 1 John 3:1–3).

2. In light of your answer to the above, answer this question: What, specifically, does the Lord want your wife to become? In practical terms, what would spiritual maturity look like for your wife? Who will your wife increasingly look like as she grows spiritually?

3. As a husband, what is your role in the Lord's process of conforming your wife to the likeness of His Son?

4. Imagine saying to your wife, "Follow my example, as I follow the example of Christ" (1 Corinthians 11:1). If that seems awkward, discuss why. What would it take for you to be able to say that to your wife with humble confidence?

Action Steps

1. Pray, if you will, "Father, I want my wife to be able to say at my funeral, 'I am more like Jesus today than I was on our wedding day because of my husband's purposeful, loving involvement in my life over the years.' Lord, please move in my life that I might be faithful in this holy quest."

2. Leading your wife toward Christlikeness assumes that you also are progressively becoming more and more like Him. What is your plan for your own spiritual growth? If you don't have a plan or only a haphazard one, then lay out a realistic, yet stretching plan this week for your own regular "spiritual workout." And get started!

3. This week, if you haven't already done so, discuss with your wife a plan for the two of you to spend time, reading and discussing God's Word and praying together.

8

A Providing
Love

I brushed my teeth today. "So, what's the big deal?" you ask. Well, if I didn't brush my teeth it might be a big deal. And I'm not referring merely to those who may have the misfortune to stand close enough to detect my bad breath. If I gave my toothbrush a vacation, eventually I would have a mouthful of unsightly decayed teeth and a host of related maladies.

Actually, I brush my teeth several times each day. Not only that, but nearly every day I take a shower, too. I take vitamins and try to eat a relatively healthful diet (as long as Dutch Apple pie qualifies as a fruit). I exercise appropriately for a guy in his fifties, and I see my doctor for an annual physical even though parts of that ordeal are less than enjoyable.

Why do I do all these things? Let me assure you I'm not on some deluded quest to be a model for the local fitness club's web site. In the words of my insightful adult son, "Dad, for you, athleticism is a distant memory!" (I think he has the gift of trying to keep his father a bit more humble.) There's no hidden agenda behind my health routines. To be frank, I try to take care of myself, well, because I love myself.

Don't get the wrong idea. I'm not into some narcissistic fawning before the balding image staring back at me from the mirror. Though still fighting vanity, I'm too old to have any desire to linger any longer than necessary before that brutally truthful bathroom mirror. But I do care about how I feel and function physically. So I exercise. I take showers. I eat oatmeal. I brush my teeth (in that order, by the way).

Am I all that different from other guys? The Apostle Paul said, "After all, no one ever hated his own body, but he feeds and cares for it" (Ephesians 5:29). We all look after our own welfare to some degree. That's just everyday human experience.

Interestingly, Paul uses this natural bent of daily caring for our bodies as an object lesson for husbands. Even more interestingly, he raises the issue above the mundane and draws our attention to the Perfect Husband, Jesus Christ.

Christ's Loving Provision for His "Body"

One of the beautiful analogies Paul uses for the church, in addition to our being His bride, is that we are His body. "You are the body of Christ, and each one of you is a part of it," he writes (1 Corinthians 12:27). We, the church, are vitally connected to Christ who serves as our "Head." In Ephesians 5:23 Paul teaches that "the husband is the head of the wife as Christ is the head of the church, his body, of which he is the Savior."

As the loving Head, Jesus Christ takes excellent care of His body, the church. He is the Perfect Provider. He "feeds and cares for" the church (Ephesians 5:29). Those two terms are sometimes used to describe the tender care of children. The first word, *feeds*, also could be translated *nurture*. The second word, translated *cares for* in the NIV, comes from a word that means "to comfort, cherish, or warm."

According to one Bible commentator, this "imagery as applied to Christ's treatment of the Church is meant to recall his constant provision for and building up of his body."[1] And Dr. Harold Hoehner assures us, "Even with all its imperfections Christ nurtures and takes tender care of his body, the church. Christ does not give birth to the church and leave it stranded. He nurses her with the warmth of his love and power so that she will be able to cope in the world."[2]

It's true, isn't it? Jesus takes good care of us! "His divine power has given us everything we need for life and godliness through our knowledge of him who called us by his own glory and goodness" (2

Peter 1:3). What comes to your mind when you think about Jesus lovingly providing everything we need to live for Him as His body? He provides forgiveness of sins, the promise of eternal life, inexpressible joy, the Holy Spirit, spiritual gifts, leaders for the church, the fellowship of other believers, and on and on we could go! He is the Perfect Provider for us, His body, His bride.

I find such encouragement in the verbal picture of Christ that Thomas Watson painted back in the 1660s: "He brings fresh supplies to his spouse. If she wanders out of the way, he guides her. If she stumbles, he holds her by the hand. If she falls, he raises her. If she is dull, he quickens her by his Spirit. If she is perverse, he draws her with cords of love. If she is sad, he comforts her with promises."[3] What a Perfect Provider is our "Husband!"

Our Loving Provision for Our "Body"

Using this double analogy—our everyday loving provision for our own physical bodies and Christ's perfect loving provision for His body, His bride, the church—Paul says we husbands are to love our wives "as [our] own bodies. He who loves his wife loves himself. After all, no one ever hated his own body, but he feeds and cares for it, just as Christ does the church—for we are members of his body" (Ephesians 5:28–30). Paul then adds this reinforcing summary, "Each one of you also must love his wife as he loves himself" (v. 33).[4]

Have you ever heard a man introducing his wife as "my better half?" That's more than a polite expression. It's reality. In this pivotal passage on marriage, Paul reaches back to Moses' comments in Genesis 2:24 regarding God's institution of the husband-wife relationship and quotes, "The two will become one flesh" (v. 31). Our wives really are our "other halves." Dr. Martyn Lloyd-Jones explains the principle this way: "A man loves his wife as his body—that is what he is saying. Not 'as' he loves his body so must he love his wife. No! a man must love his wife as his body, as part of himself. As Eve was a part of Adam, taken out of his side, so the wife is to the man, because she is a part of him."[5]

We husbands must not think of ourselves individualistically, as if we were somehow whole in and of ourselves. If we could somehow view ourselves separately from our wives, we would see that we are, in fact, "halves." Our wives are our *other* halves who, when joined to us, make us whole. We and our wives are divinely joined by God into one united whole.

Isn't this what Jesus said when rebuking the Pharisees for their low view of the permanence of marriage? He also reached back to Genesis 2:24:

> "Haven't you read," he replied, "that at the beginning the Creator 'made them male and female,' and said, 'For this reason a man will leave his father and mother and be united to his wife, and the two will become one flesh'? So they are no longer two, but one. Therefore what God has joined together, let man not separate" (Matthew 19:4–6).

This divinely orchestrated oneness or wholeness of the marriage union may explain why those going through divorce often express their profound pain as "I feel like I'm being ripped apart." In a sense, they are.

Considering this imagery, think about Paul's observation in Ephesians 5:28: "He who loves his wife loves himself." In other words, what the husband does for his wife, he is, in a sense, doing for himself. He is benefited in benefiting her. John Ensor writes, "When she is fulfilled in her life, I am full and rich indeed. This is the very essence of love, the true heart of the matter. This is how it is that 'the two shall become one flesh.'"[6]

Lately I've been mulling over this comment by Jesus, "Where your treasure is, there your heart will be also" (Matthew 6:21). People often think of Jesus' words in the reverse of what He actually said. Many assume that Jesus was observing that we tend to invest in whatever is important to us—that we tend to put our time, energy, and money into whatever we highly value.

But what He actually said is the flip side of that maxim. Jesus said that our hearts—our values—will follow our investments. For example, if you were to put a major portion of your nest egg into a particular stock, you would find yourself with an increased concern about the financial health of that investment. You would regularly check that stock in the newspaper financial section or bookmark that stock's web site in your "favorites" list. The value you place on that stock would increase in proportion to the amount you invest.

While Jesus did not directly apply this proverb to marriage, I've been wondering how it fits. If I invest the majority of my time, thoughts, and energy in my work, my hobbies, or even my ministries, I will find my heart going in those directions. The more I invest in those things, the more I will care about them.

Sadly, if I am investing significantly in those areas, I am probably neglecting my wife—my "body." My paltry "deposits" of time, thought, and energy invested in her diminish her value in my heart. Neglecting her—devaluing her—hurts her. And since she is "my other half"—my "body"—it also hurts me.

We husbands are not doing ourselves any favor by neglecting our wives. But in "treasuring" them, there is great reward.

So how do we husbands show Christlike love for our wives by investing in them? And what can we provide for our wives that would benefit them—and us?

Providing Financial Stability

While we have no guarantee of the ongoing financial health of our places of employment, our region, or even our nation, we husbands should do what we can to provide financially for our wives and our families. Admittedly, some men cannot provide adequately for their families for a season because of the loss of their health or their jobs. But in the Lord's normal providence a man should do whatever he can to provide financially for the care of his family. First Timothy 5:8 boldly states, "If anyone does not provide for his relatives, and especially for his immediate family, he has denied the faith and is worse than an unbeliever."

Is your wife assured that you love her and are committed to sacrificially demonstrating that love by providing for her financial and material needs? John Piper put it this way:

> A man compromises his own soul and sends the wrong message to his wife and children when he does not position himself as the one who lays down his life to put bread on the table. He may be disabled and unable to do what his

heart longs to do. He may be temporarily in school while she supports the family. But in any case his heart, and, if possible, his body, is moving toward the use of his mind and his hands to provide physically for his wife and children.[7]

Often a husband fails to lovingly provide financial stability for his wife's peace of mind because he carelessly spends the family's money on his own self-gratifying pursuits. Patrick Morley writes, "Today men are consumed by desires to buy things they don't need, with money they don't have, to impress people they don't like."[8]

How many wives have felt the stress of trying to make the family's finances stretch to meet monthly bills while their husbands have been spending money selfishly on their toys, such as unnecessary vehicles, expensive golf clubs, costly hunting gear, or the latest electronic devices—often by using credit cards with exorbitant interest rates?

Men, let's model the sacrificial love of Christ by gladly forgoing our own desires and providing for our wives whatever financial stability we can.

Providing Emotional Security

Many wives struggle with their sense of personal value. This fallen world can beat up on our wives' sense of their worth as image bearers of our great and glorious Creator. They are bombarded by advertisements depicting women with "perfect" bodies. They are assaulted by talk shows and magazine articles that present this world's "ideal" woman. Those who have elected to be stay-at-home moms are assailed by the unsolicited opinions of friends and relatives regarding what they "could be doing with their lives."

We husbands are primary instruments in God's gracious hands, providing our wives emotional security and reminding them of their great value in God's sight and ours. Peter exhorts us, "Husbands, in the same way be considerate as you live with your wives, *and treat them with respect* as the weaker partner and as heirs with you of the gracious gift of life, so that nothing will hinder your prayers" (1 Peter 3:7, emphasis added). The idea is to assign your wife a position of honor. So how do we do that?

1. Appreciation. We can honor her by providing word
appreciation. Craig Peters gives us this humorous ch
moment some evening when you're lying in bed anu ....
three things you appreciate about her. If she faints in the process,
that's a good sign you need to be affirming her more."[9] Guys, let's
make it a habit to lovingly provide our wives emotional security by
showing appreciation as often as we can, for example:

> "Honey, that was a great meal. Thanks so much for your
> hard work in preparing it."

> "Sweetheart, thank you so much for all you do to make our
> house a home."

> "You are such a great mother to our children. Thank you for
> your sacrifice."

> Or how about this one? "Wow! You are one amazing lover!
> Thank you!"

2. Admiration. We can also honor our wives by providing words
and tokens of admiration. Derek Prince writes, "Some husbands are
stingy with their words of praise. That is false economy! They would
be surprised to discover how much a wife longs to be praised—and
how she responds to it. Giving praise to your wife is one of the best
investments you can ever make."[10] What does Proverbs 31 say about
the husband of the wife of noble character? "Her husband…praises
her: 'Many women do noble things, but you surpass them all'" (vv.
28–29).

Men, what is it you admire about your wife? Give it some
thought. Something about her appearance? Her character? Her gifts
or accomplishments? "Invest" in your wife by tenderly speaking your
words of admiration directly to her and praising her to others—especially in her presence. You can also minister to her by writing
encouraging notes to her.

Let's banish forever any jokes about "my old woman" or "my old
lady." Once again drawing a comparison with Christ and His bride,
Dean Merrill pointedly observes, "I imagine Christ could crack quite
a lot of very funny jokes about the imperfections of the church. But
he doesn't. He loves us too much."[11]

Your wife is a precious gift from God, and she's your fellow heir of God's gracious gift of life. Treat her that way.

3. *Assurance of her value.* We also assign our wives positions of honor when we give them words and tokens of assurance.

- Listening to your wife's concerns attentively and responding with care and interest assures her that you highly value her and her feelings.

- Giving her time, your most precious commodity, assures her that you value her. Often, the most assuring act of love you can give your wife is a tender, unhurried hug when you sense she is discouraged.

- Making yourself accessible to her at all times assures her that you care about every aspect of her life. It provides emotional security. Make sure she knows that she is so highly valued in your heart and eyes, she is always free to call you at any time. I have established a personal policy with our office staff that if Gladine calls, I will take her call no matter what I am doing. I value her that much, and I want to assure her of that by being accessible.

Providing Spiritual Strengthening

In *The Christian Husband,* Bob Lepine refers to a Puritan pastor, Samuel Davies, who observed that Christian men don't take their full responsibility as providers. "Davies…wondered why we are we so quick to care for those material needs, which are not eternal, while we ignore the spiritual needs of our wives and our families, which will endure forever? In an era driven by material gain and workaholism, it's a sobering question."[12]

There is more on this important subject in chapter 7, "A Purposeful Love," but I think it's wise at least to mention here that this is another loving provision we can make for our wives. We husbands need to be aware of our wives' spiritual needs and provide for them with Christlike love.

Providing Social Stimulus

Let's face it, guys. Our wives often think differently than we do. So we need to humble ourselves continually, asking ourselves this question: What is it that my wife longs for as evidence of my love? Dean Merrill dares us to give our wives this multiple-choice quiz:

> The greatest evidence that my husband loves me is that:
> ❑ He spends money on me.
> ❑ He gives great sex.
> ❑ He talks [to me]."[13]

What do you think would be the most common answer wives give? You bet! Our wives crave for us to interact with them, to talk with them.

No doubt this is true in all seasons of marriage, but it may be especially important during those years when our wives are occupied all day with preschoolers. Our wives want us to listen to them and to interact with them in a socially stimulating way. Even if you find yourself tired after a long day at work and the stresses of a long commute, with Christlike, sacrificial love, make the time to converse with your wife in a way that shows you truly care about what she's talking about.

Remember that old rule we learned years ago in driver's training class about approaching railroad crossings? Stop, look, and listen.

Stop. Turn off the TV. Lay down the newspaper.

Look. Look into her eyes with your face communicating loving interest.

Listen. I mean actively listen. Learn to ask questions that draw her out, that invite her to share not only events of the day but her feelings about them.

Lou Priolo writes, "When you're willing to talk to your wife about the things that interest her (no matter how trivial or uninteresting they may be to you), you'll be demonstrating a Christ-like, sacrificial love that makes it easier for her to open up to you."[14]

Providing Sexual Satisfaction

This is one ministry to our wives that is ours and ours alone. No one else on the face of this earth is ordained of God to provide sexual satisfaction for our wives. That satisfaction comes when we, as loving husbands, touch our wives' hearts and then their bodies. Paul says plainly, "The husband should fulfill his marital duty to his wife...The husband's body does not belong to him alone but also to his wife" (1 Corinthians 7:3–4). As we express our love to our wives sexually, may we husbands find our greatest joy by bringing *our wives* satisfaction in body and heart. For more on this important (and fascinating!) subject, be sure to carefully read Chapter 9, "A Passionate Love."

With our eyes on The Perfect Provider, recalling how natural it is for us to care for our own bodies, let's love our wives with a Christlike providing love. "He who loves his wife loves himself" (Ephesians 5:28).

DISCUSSION QUESTIONS AND ACTION STEPS
A Providing Love

Discussion Questions

1. Read Ephesians 5:28–29. Jesus shows love for His bride by feeding and caring for her. What are some ways that Jesus demonstrates this providing love? Start a list of some things Jesus provides for us.

2. Jesus said, "Where your treasure is, there your heart will be also" (Matthew 6:21). What's His point? How might this principle apply to how much we invest in our relationship with our wives?

3. List some ways husbands can be more diligent in providing financial stability in their marriages. (See 1 Timothy 5:8.) In our culture, financial instability is more often caused by unwise or uncontrolled spending than insufficient income. Are there some areas of your own spending habits ("toys," gambling, drinking, misuse of credit cards, and so forth) that you need to change? How can the guys in your group help you make changes in this area of your life so you can be a better loving, providing husband?

4. Why is it often a challenge to give our wives social stimulus by having meaningful conversations with them on a regular basis? What might help?

Action Steps

1. When you get home from work each day this week, take a few minutes to process with your wife how her day has gone. This might best be done by talking as you prepare dinner together. Ask her questions not only about her activities but how she felt about her day.

2. Make a point each day this week to offer your wife some words of appreciation or admiration for something she has done or for some Christlike character trait she has demonstrated. Compliment her on some aspect of her appearance. (See Proverbs 31:28–31.)

9

A Passionate
Love

Gladine and I enjoy walking a couple miles together through our neighborhood in the morning. It gives us a little exercise and some uninterrupted time to talk. One day as we were walking, Gladine gave me some encouraging input on my sermon from the previous Sunday. "Larry, those personal illustrations from your own life are so helpful," she said. "I think you should use personal illustrations more often when you preach. What are you preaching on this coming Sunday?"

With a grin I told her the truth, "Sexual relations in marriage."

After the briefest of pauses, Gladine responded, "I take it all back! I take back everything I said about using personal illustrations!"

I was careful not to embarrass my precious Gladine unnecessarily by using personal illustrations from our love life when I preached from 1 Corinthians 7 the following Sunday. As much as I have found soul-touching, breathtaking pleasure in the intimacy we have shared in our more than 30 years of marriage, I will honor her similarly in this chapter on passionate love.

Understandably, details about a married couple's most intimate moments are not to be shared with anyone else. They are ours—and ours alone—to revel in together, to remember with great delight, and to relish with eager anticipation. Yet God never put the discussion of passionate sex in marriage on some taboo list. In fact, right at the beginning of His book He speaks of the first couple—and all subsequent married couples—as becoming "one flesh" (Genesis 2:24).

God's Word also includes rather explicit fatherly counsel to a young married son regarding sex: "Drink water from your own cistern, running water from your own well...May your fountain be blessed, and may you rejoice in the wife of your youth. A loving doe, a graceful deer—may her breasts satisfy you always, may you ever be captivated by her love" (Proverbs 5:15–19).

Do I hear an amen?

Consider the Song of Solomon. Wow! Have you read that part of the Bible lately? While never vulgar, it is poetically explicit in recounting the passionate sexual intimacy enjoyed by the kingly author and his bride.

Rather than treating the Song of Solomon as some sort of embarrassingly less-than-spiritual piece of poetry that somehow sneaked into the list of canonical books, husbands can read it in light of 2 Timothy 3:16–17: "All Scripture [including the Song of Solomon] is God-breathed and is useful for teaching, rebuking, correcting and training in righteousness [including the Song of Solomon], so that the man of God may be thoroughly equipped for every good work [even making love to your wife in a way that not only brings her great pleasure but which reflects the glory of God!]" (bracketed material mine).

So read the Song of Solomon. In fact, try this challenge given by a speaker I heard at a marriage retreat: "Men, with your wife already in bed, sit on the edge of the bed and read aloud to her from the Song of Solomon. At the group breakfast in the morning, tell me how far you got!"

Now, there's a homework assignment, men!

God not only directed the biblical authors to depict passionate love between husband and wife, but He actually commands husbands and wives to have regular and mutually satisfying sexual relations (1 Corinthians 7:5)! God *wants us* to be passionate lovers to our wives.

But what happened to our analogy of Christ and the church? Is it okay to picture God as having passionate love for us, His church?

Christ's Passionate Love for His Bride

This question may seem like it comes out of nowhere, but "Does God sing?" Maybe the question sounds like something from a curious five-year-old whose mind has wandered during family devotions. But let's not dismiss it too quickly. How would you answer that question? Can you think of any examples in the Bible of God singing? How about Zephaniah 3:17? "The LORD your God is with you...he will quiet you with his love, he will rejoice over you with singing."

Does God sing? Yes! And notice what moves the heart of God to sing: He rejoices over us, His people!

Let's eavesdrop, as it were, as Dr. John Piper preaches on this passage from the often-neglected book of Zephaniah:

> Can you imagine what it would be like if you could hear God singing? Remember that it was merely a spoken word that brought the universe into existence. What would happen if God lifted up his voice and not only spoke but also sang! Perhaps a new heaven and a new earth would be created. God says something almost...to that effect in Isaiah 65:17–18....And when I hear this singing, I stand dumbfounded, staggered, speechless that he is singing over me. He is rejoicing over my good with all his heart and with all his soul! Can you feel the wonder of this today? That God is rejoicing over you with loud singing?"[1]

One evening when I arrived home from the office, a tenderhearted young lady who had been living under the dark clouds of depression for some time was sitting at our kitchen table. Gladine was seeking to share God's grace with this sensitive younger sister in Christ who so desperately wanted to please the Lord but felt she never lived up to His expectations.

At my wife's request I joined their conversation. I asked this young lady one question. "Is God smiling at you or frowning at you?"

I could see in her eyes the desperate desire to say the word *smiling*. But I could also see the disbelief that it could ever be true in her case. So I pointed her to Christ and His all-sufficient work on the cross on our behalf. I explained that in those dark Calvary hours, God poured out onto Jesus every single drop of wrath we deserved for our sinful rebellion. Jesus absorbed it all, and now not an atom of God's condemnation remains for us, His people. Because of Jesus Christ, God now smiles on us. That news brought a million-dollar smile to the face of this young lady. There were tears of joy all around that kitchen table as we reveled together in God's incredible grace. John Piper says,

> We must banish from our minds forever any thought that God admits us begrudgingly into his Kingdom, as though Christ found a loophole in the law, did some fancy plea-bargaining and squeaked us by the Judge. No way! God himself, the Judge, put Christ forward as our substitutionary sacrifice, and when we trust him, *God* welcomes us with bells on. He puts a ring on our finger, kills the fatted calf, throws a party, shouts a shout that shakes the ends of creation, and leads in the festal dance.[2]

The Lord smiles at us. The Lord sings over us. He loves us with passionate love. Jesus loves His bride, the church, intensely.

Let me clarify: While I'm not proposing that we think of Christ's love for the church as being erotic or sexual, neither do I think we should shrink from using words of passion to describe Christ's love for us.

It may seem that using sexual terminology or examples goes too far in depicting the love Christ has for His bride. But I wonder if it's actually going far enough. As powerful and as passionate as marital love is (Song of Solomon 8:6 says it's "as strong as death"), the inexpressibly intense sexual expression of the love a husband has for his wife is but an imperfect representation of Christ's perfect, powerful, passionate love for His bride, the church.

I realize most of you have already figured out this chapter is about *sex*, and you're wishing I'd get on with "the good stuff." Let me assure you that if we are going to better understand how to passionately and intimately love our wives, we need to study our Model, the Perfect Husband—the Perfectly Passionate Husband, Jesus Christ—and His love for His bride.

Jesus is preparing for His glorious, sure-coming wedding day with great anticipation. Listen to the passion of the apostle John's prophetic account of that day:

> Then I heard what sounded like a great multitude, like the roar of rushing waters and like loud peals of thunder, shouting: "Hallelujah! For our Lord God Almighty reigns. Let us rejoice and be glad and give him glory! For the wedding of the Lamb has come, and his bride has made herself ready"… Then the angel said to me…"Blessed are those who are invited to the wedding supper of the Lamb!" (Revelation 19:6–7, 9).

Hundreds of years before Jesus came to earth to redeem His bride, God had prophesied this glorious relationship of passionate intimacy through Old Testament prophets. "As a bridegroom rejoices over his bride, so will your God rejoice over you" (Isaiah 62:5). Regarding this heartening promise, Bible scholar Dr. E. J. Young writes, "He will rejoice in her as an earthly bridegroom rejoices in his bride. This figure is designed to express the utmost of rejoicing."[3]

John Ensor elaborates: "God's delight in his Bride causes him to plan and pursue us just as a man pursues the one great love of his life. This in turn becomes the model or example for what we are after in our own intimate relationship."[4]

A few pages later in our Bibles we read of God's promised passionate joy in His people: "Be glad and rejoice forever in what I will create, for I will create Jerusalem to be a delight and its people a joy. I will rejoice over Jerusalem and take delight in my people" (Isaiah 65:18–19). Is God smiling on us, His bride? No fewer than six times in this short passage God expresses the idea of His joy. John Calvin emphasizes that the Lord's love for us is so great that "God is moved…powerfully moved, by such an affection toward us"![5]

On the night before the cross, Jesus spoke of His passionate love for His people. "Greater love has no one than this, that he lay down his life for his friends" (John 15:13). Yes, it's true that His love was a "decided" love—an act of the will. But it was more than that. It was also a love of affection, of emotion, of passion. In His passion at Gethsemane and at Calvary, Jesus unquestionably revealed the intensity of His love for His church.

So when Paul says, "Husbands, love your wives, just as Christ loved the church" (Ephesians 5:25), he's not speaking merely of the decided love of our wills but the passionate love of our affections.

Our Passionate Love for Our Wives

Remember courting your wife? For some, those memories are very recent. For others decades of life have come and gone since those days when our love was just beginning to bloom.

Either way, what do you remember? Talking with her for what seemed but a few minutes, only to discover that hours had gone by? Many letters (or e-mails) exchanged during a season of separation, expressing your painful longing to be together? Laughing at each other's antics with the giddiness of youthful love? Spontaneously chasing each other through the park? Making angels in the snow? The first kiss?

What comes to mind when you reflect on your honeymoon? The excitement of (finally!) getting away from wedding guests blowing bubbles or throwing birdseed (or for us "oldsters," rice) at you and your bride at the end of the reception? Of being alone—really alone—at last? The excitement of seeing your bride for the first time in her honeymoon nightgown? The even greater excitement of seeing your bride for the first time *without* her honeymoon nightgown? Feeling a bit clumsy at making love on your wedding night, but not really caring because you were finally *together*?

Good memories, aren't they? But those fires of passion that once burned so hot, how high are the flames these days? Do you find your conversations with your wife more clipped these days, focusing primarily on responsibilities of kids, jobs, and keeping the house in running order? Have your kisses become little perfunctory pecks as you go off to work in the morning? Is the only laughter in your bedroom coming from the TV, droning on from the late-night show, long after you have drifted off in weary boredom?

Has your lovemaking become less frequent and more predictable? What if those barely glowing embers could somehow be rekindled into passionate ardor? Sound too good to be true?

What if that's what God wants?

I heartily support Dennis Rainey's optimistic outlook when he writes, "I'm convinced God wants your romance to blossom and grow, not shrivel up and become nonexistent; He wants you to experience great sex, satisfying oneness, and a whole new level of intimacy you never dreamed possible."[6]

If God really does want our marriages to blaze with passionate love, isn't it possible—even likely—that He has already given us the direction and grace needed to stir the fire? If this is His will, then what has He provided to make it happen?

Passionate Romance

What comes to your mind when you read the word *foreplay?* If you are like me—and, no doubt, 99.99% of all other men—it's *sex.* Hormone-charged images of intimately arousing our wives rush to our minds. Just hearing or reading the word *foreplay* tempts us to lay down this book and go find our wives. Men seem to be able to think about sex without even thinking about it, if you know what I mean.

Much to the confusion of our wives, we husbands can feel ready to have sex with our wives just about anywhere, anytime. And we can get perturbed if our wives don't respond with the same fervor. Feeling rebuffed, it seems our flames of passion just got lowered from high to simmer.

What's going on here? The apostle Peter counseled, "Husbands… be considerate as you live with your wives" (1 Peter 3:7). A literal rendition of *considerate* is "according to knowledge." In other words, the Bible says that we are supposed to understand our wives! And, in case you haven't noticed, your wife is not like you.

Oh, she's different anatomically (isn't God good?), but she's also different in how she looks at life, how she looks at marriage, and, yes, how she looks at sex. Men tend to compartmentalize their lives. Work fits in this compartment, family in that one, hobbies over here, church over there. Often men don't see the connection between compartments. That is true even with sex.

We might have left for work in the morning with an unresolved conflict still sitting like an elephant in our kitchen. Yet we can come home that evening, hormones charging, and not understand why our wives aren't as ready as we are to get the kids down early so we can rush off to our bed for some passionate lovemaking. We may ask, "How does some silly argument hours before have anything to do with getting some serious pillow time as husband and wife? Why is my wife holding that over my head at a time like this?" Again, what's going on here?

Do you really want to know? Feeling gutsy? Why not ask your wife what comes to her mind when *she* hears the word *foreplay*? Maybe ask her this way: "Honey, in your ideal world, when would foreplay start?" Don't be surprised if her answer points to a time before the clothes come off. A generation ago, Dr. Ed Wheat advised, "Husband, you should be aware that your wife views the sex act as part of her total relationship with you, even though you, like other men, may think of it separately."[7]

Why is this? If we go back to the very beginning, we see that God created the first wife, Eve, in such a way that she complemented Adam. God made Eve for relationship with her husband. It is only because we forget God's design for women that we husbands are mystified when our wives refuse to look at life through our compartmentalized eyes, wanting instead to tie everything together. In their God-designed outlook that unresolved breakfast conflict has everything to do with why they are not ready to jump into the sack with us at our not-so-subtle husbandly come-ons.

Remember the question we want to ask our wives? "What comes to your mind when you hear the word *foreplay*?" Her answer is probably much broader than ours. While men would probably answer with the specific word, *sex*, I wouldn't be surprised if our wives answer with the broader word, *romance*.

Men, let's humble ourselves, seeking to understand and serve our wives as God designed them to be, rather than pressuring them to think and act like us. Let's go to our Creator, learning from His Word how to romance these precious wives He has blessed us with. By God's grace and for His glory, with Christlike passionate love, let us learn how to once again stir the fires of passion in our marriages.

Here's a memorable life lesson for us husbands from Sovereign Grace Ministries leader C. J. Mahaney's insightful book, *Sex, Romance, and the Glory of God*: "In order for romance to deepen, you must touch the heart and mind of your wife before you touch her body."[8] Maybe we should inscribe a plaque with these words and hang it in our bedroom. Maybe create a screen saver with those words—assuming you are the only one who uses that computer!

Seriously, every husband needs to memorize this maxim: Touch the heart and mind of your wife before you touch her body. Mahaney emphasizes it again: "Nothing kindles erotic romance in a marriage like a husband who knows how to touch the heart and mind of his wife before he touches her body."[9]

So, you ask, how do I touch her mind and heart?

Good question. Answer? Romance her.

Don't feel you're a gifted romantic? You're not alone. In the words of Gary and Betsy Ricucci, "Romance must be continually practiced, like an art. The basic tools that you as a budding artist must bring to your craft include a heart of humility, a spirit of servanthood, a biblical understanding of marriage, and a fervent desire to know and love your spouse as consistently and creatively as possible."[10]

We need to humble ourselves, men, and recognize that most of us have a lot to learn about the art of romancing our wives. I recommend two resources:

1. Ask your wife what makes her feel that you love her or what you could do to make her feel loved.

2. Study the Song of Solomon, God's inspired model of a husband passionately romancing his wife.

Romance Involves Talking

Notice in the Song of Solomon how the husband (the lover) uses tender, passionate words to woo his wife's heart and mind —long before he touches her body. Mahaney writes, "A clear lesson from Solomon's Song is that speech and sex are intimately connected."[11]

The artful lover repeatedly calls her "my darling." He describes her beauty (see Song of Solomon chapter 4). Using creatively descriptive analogies, he tells her how her beauty stirs his passion. And he tells her of his longing for her: "Show me your face, let me hear your voice; for your voice is sweet, and your face is lovely" (Song of Solomon 2:14).

Though you and I might not want to use the same analogies Solomon used 3,000 years ago, we can, nevertheless, practice the art of romancing our wives with *our* tender words. Hold her face in your hands, gaze into her eyes, and tell her how beautiful she is to you and how glad you are that God blessed you with her as your wife. Tell her you value her more than any other person on this earth.

C. J. Mahaney again emphasizes, "Communication and sex are inseparable. It's not as though sex is one thing and communication is something else. Life doesn't divide into neat little compartments like that, especially when it comes to the oneness of marriage. It's all one thing. It's all…intercourse."[12] He adds, "What we express toward our wives and how we behave toward our wives in the days and hours before we make love is actually far more important than what we do when the clothes come off….[Our wives] know that carefully composed words have great power to promote romance and marital intimacy. Many of us husbands, sad to say, don't have a clue."[13]

Of course, some of our daily conversation as husbands and wives is fact oriented: "What would you like for dinner?" or "Can you pick up the kids after practice?" However, romantic talk moves beyond facts to the heart, to feelings and emotions—both wife's and husband's. To romance our wives, we'll want to push aside all distractions, look into her eyes and engage her emotionally.

Dennis Rainey recommends this: "Cradle her face in your hands and tell her that she causes your heart to beat faster…that you love making love to her…that you can't get enough of her voice. Praise her for the 'little things' she does as your wife—and be specific. Then with a twinkle in your eye, tell her you would marry her all over again."[14] Good advice, isn't it, men?

While the ideal is to be able to speak directly to your wife while looking into her eyes, you can touch your wife's mind and heart with your words even when you are not physically together. Spontaneously call her from work or from a business trip, telling her how much you miss her and how you can hardly wait to be with her. Send her a quick e-mail from your desk, letting her know how much you love her. Leave her a card or note where she will find it later in the day, telling her of your love and how you will be praying for her during your day. The results may surprise you.

Romance Involves Time

How much do you truly value your wife? Does she know? We make time for what we value most. So you may need to invest more time in your wife to show you how much she means to you. Over time, you will find your heart following your investment (Matthew 6:21), and your love for your wife will continue to grow year after year.

Make time to be with her—really *with* her, no distractions. What she craves is a relationship with you. Don't merely pursue *sex* from your wife. Pursue *her.*

Dennis Rainey says that if we feel our wives are not that excited about our sexual advances, we may need to evaluate how much we've been investing in our relationship. "Her heart can be like a bank account where you make deposits and withdrawals," he writes. "Far too often as men we can make withdrawals and disregard making deposits or investments."[15]

Does your wife know, by the amount of time you invest in your *friendship*, that you treasure her? "Romance is, after all," Rainey says, "like a friendship that has been set on fire."[16]

Romance Involves Touching

Our touches should mean something. I mean, more than signaling we want sex from our wives. Our touches can communicate the high value we put on our wives and how much we enjoy just being close. What kind of touches does your wife especially enjoy? What kind of touches reassure her of your undying love?

- Hold her hand. Scratch her back. Rub her tired feet. Give her a massage.
- Run your fingers through her hair. Even better, comb her hair.
- Invite her to sit on your lap. Put your arm around her. Snuggle on the couch.
- Touch her affectionately and say something sweet as you walk by.
- Snuggle in bed for a few minutes before crawling out to begin the day.
- Kiss—sometimes lightly, sometimes passionately.
- Always greet her with a hug and kiss when you come home.

Romance Involves Thoughtful Actions

Little things count. One time I was telling the guys in my account-ability group that our marriage was in a valley. My wife seemed disappointed with me, and I was frustrated with her lack of enthusiasm over my "husbanding." I guess I was hoping for some sympathy, but I presented it, of course, in the form of a request for prayer support.

Instead, what I received from my buds was a brotherly confrontation. They asked me if I was showing love to Gladine in daily little ways—ways that made her feel special. Was I romancing my wife every day through thoughtful actions? The guys were right in challenging me. Romance involves more than expensive getaways and great sex. Those daily, thoughtful expressions of love are an important means of romancing our wives. Need some ideas? Here are a few suggestions that may spark ideas of your own:

- Keep a photo of your wife, or of the two of you together, on your desk or workbench. Let her know that you enjoy having this regular reminder of her at your workplace and that you enjoy putting your coworkers on notice that she is supremely important to you.

- Give her gifts. Even as Christ gives good gifts to His bride (spiritual gifts, church leaders, and more), we can show our love for our wives by giving them meaningful gifts. Pay attention to what pleases her. Study her. Ask her. And keep a list of gift ideas in your wallet or on your PDA! Gifts don't have to cost a lot. If you're on a tight budget, be creative!

- Leave a special private note on her pillow letting her know how much you appreciate her and enjoy being alone with her.

- Ask a relative or friend to take the kids for an evening, giving you and your wife an evening at home alone. Make it special for her, not just something you would enjoy as a guy. Maybe instead of having pizza while watching your favorite sport on TV, plan a candlelight dinner and soft background music that your wife would enjoy.

- Remember special events, especially her birthday and your wedding anniversary. Plan ahead. Don't leave the planning to your wife even if you feel she's better at it.

- Plan "dates" and romantic getaways as your budget allows. Keep a list of ideas of places to go and things to do.

Passionate Sex

Sex is God's idea. And, as we have already discussed, isn't He kind in giving us the Song of Solomon as part of the Bible? C. J. Mahaney says that book is "an eight-chapter feast of unbridled, uninhibited, joyous immersion in verbal and physical expressions of passion between a man and a woman. Not a couple of verses. Not a chapter or two. God didn't consider that enough. He decided to give us a whole book!"[17]

We should revel in God's kindness in giving us both the gift of marital sex and directions for using this amazingly joyful gift.

Right from the beginning, in the first book of the Bible, God's Word unashamedly acknowledges that he created Adam and Eve to be sexual creatures. Carolyn Mahaney writes, "God did not wince when Adam, in seeing Eve, was drawn to her sexually. God didn't cringe when Adam and Eve enjoyed sexual relations in the Garden of Eden. In His wise and perfect design, he gave sexual desire to both the man and the woman."[18]

Carolyn Mahaney's husband, C. J., adds:

> Sex is…meant to accomplish several key purposes: union…intimacy…comfort, pleasure, and play…creation of life…protection from sexual temptation. Sexual intercourse and those wonderfully intense passions it brings about are designed to help man and wife form a relational bond of unique, unparalleled richness. When these divine purposes are experienced and fulfilled, they bring much glory to God.[19]

Sex Is a Matter of Giving, Not Just Getting

Husbands need to be careful not to treat their wives as some sort of sex objects whose job is to keep them satisfied. Author Lou Priolo says, "Probably the greatest way that Christian husbands fail in the sexual part of their marriage is by being selfish. We live in an auto-erotic society. That is, a society that views sex primarily as something from which pleasure is to be received, rather than as an opportunity for which pleasure can be given."[20]

I remember a young couple who came to me for pastoral counseling some time ago. They hadn't been married long, but already they were struggling. I can still recall the pain on her face and the oblivion on his. Expressing many hurts, the young wife also told me she felt "used" sexually by her husband. While he looked at me blankly, she poured out her frustration. For them, she said, "lovemaking" was a five-minute exercise of his achieving a climax then rolling over and going to sleep or turning on the TV, leaving her sexually frustrated and emotionally empty. This recently saved husband had not yet broken out of the selfishness of his heart—a selfishness fueled and reinforced by the "sex-is-about-satisfying-yourself" culture in which he had operated for so long.

But I'm thankful to report that he listened as I opened my Bible and counseled him from this verse: "The husband should fulfill his marital duty to his wife" (1 Corinthians 7:3)—giving pleasure, not just getting it. Then I showed both of them that their times of intimacy were Christ-reflecting opportunities to "serve one another in love" (Galatians 5:13). And the Holy Spirit began His kind, though sometimes painful, work in this young husband's life.

The Bible is clear. If we are to love our wives as Christ loved the church, we are to reflect Christ's selfless, sacrificial love by being *givers* more than *takers* in our sexual relationships with our wives. In contrast to this world's callous treatment of women as sex objects for men to use for their own gratification, the Bible teaches husbands the God-honoring commitment of seeking *their wives'* sexual satisfaction.

Dean Merrill observes, "When…we apply the model of servanthood to this area [sex], all the dynamics change. The goal becomes the provision of her needs rather than our own. And we find, as we've noticed before, that our own needs are met along the way rather automatically."[21]

Yet this pattern of giving doesn't happen naturally, does it? We are by nature selfish takers. Maybe God designed marriage's mutual-giving dynamic as a regular reminder of how much we need His grace. It is grace that enables us to be great lovers for our wives.

God Wants Us to Enjoy Sex Regularly

Want some great news? God *wants* us to enjoy this mutually satisfying gift of sex with our wives *regularly*. In fact, He actually commands it! In 1 Corinthians 7:5, under the inspiration of the Holy Spirit, Paul instructs us, "Do not deprive each other except by mutual consent and for a time, so that you may devote yourselves to prayer. Then come together again so that Satan will not tempt you because of your lack of self-control."

Guys, beware of misusing this verse as a manipulative tool to coerce your wife to have sexual relations more often than she may desire. On the other hand, it's important to note that some wives actually desire sexual relations more frequently than their husbands. Those husbands whose wives have the stronger sex drive need to keep in mind this biblical mandate to humbly and gladly give them the sexual fulfillment they desire.

When we are thoughtfully and humbly seeking to satisfy our wives, we are a means of God's grace in their lives, providing a hedge against the temptation to commit adultery. Pastor Dave Harvey warns, "When we deprive our spouse of the adventure of sexual devotion, we leave him or her unprotected, open to physical and emotional temptations that can leave marriage vulnerable to destructive actions and habits."[22]

God Wants our Sexual Relations to Be Pure

My body does not belong to me. It belongs to my wife. Before God and more than 200 witnesses, I presented my body to her on June 21, 1975. These many years later, my body remains dedicated to her and to her sexual fulfillment. And, if you are married, I can say without reservation that this is essential for you too: Your body isn't yours. It's your wife's.

That comes right from the pages of the Bible. "The wife does not have authority over her own body, but the husband does; and likewise also *the husband does not have authority over his own body, but the wife does*" (1 Corinthians 7:4 NASB, emphasis added).

Your body is actually *hers*! Priolo writes, "When you got married, you gave up the right to use your body only as you see fit. You no longer possess sole authority over your own body—your wife does."[23]

Since, in accordance with the Word of God, your body belongs to your wife for her sexual fulfillment, you have no right to pursue self-gratification.

Taking what rightfully belongs to your wife and "spending" it with some other woman or satisfying yourself through pornography and/or masturbation is a sin not only against God but also against your wife. You are *robbing* your wife of what rightfully belongs to her according to the revealed plan of God.

God has given us such a beautiful gift to share with our wives. Let's enjoy it the way He intended.

Ideas for Becoming a Better Lover

Here are some ways to keep growing as your wife's lover:

1. If you skipped over it, go back and read the preceding section on romancing your wife, putting into practice the reality that foreplay begins long before the clothes come off!

2. Take your time! Your wife will love you for it. Commenting on the lovers in Song of Solomon chapter 4, husband-wife writing team, Cyril and Aldyth Barber note:

    > It is interesting for us, in our hurried world, to notice the time taken by this couple as they prepare themselves for sexual intercourse...Look at verse 6. It implies continuing their lovemaking until daybreak. Of course, Solomon and the Shulamite are on their honeymoon and can afford to take their time. The point...is that even when we have to rise up early the next morning, get the kids off to school, and be at the office on time, we should not hurry through our lovemaking.[24]

3. Honor your wife's desire for privacy, making sure the kids are down for the evening and that your bedroom door has a secure lock.

4. Take the time to clean up before lovemaking. It may amaze you what taking a shower, trimming your nails, and even shaving your five-o'clock shadow communicates to your wife.

5. Address any patterns of sexual difficulties you may notice. Openly and honestly evaluate possible causes. *Is it a physical problem?* Seek medical attention promptly. *Is it a technique problem?* Humble yourself, confessing your need and your desire to better understand your wife and better understand how to satisfy her sexually. Ask her what she finds pleasurable and what she does not. *Is it a sign of a spiritual or relational problem in the marriage?* This is often the cause. Humbly talk about your problems without becoming defensive. Tenderly get your wife's insight into what she believes the underlying problems may be. Then, by God's grace, seek to change in ways that would honor the Lord and strengthen your marriage.

6. Learn together as husband and wife. Read helpful books, such as the classic by Dr. Ed Wheat and his wife, Gaye, *Intended for Pleasure* and C. J. Mahaney's *Sex, Romance, and the Glory of God* (see Sources). Remember that satisfying your wife sexually is an *art* as well as a *skill.* If you will commit to becoming a humble learner, you should become a better lover over time, so practice, practice, practice!

7. Thank your wife regularly, consistently, for making love with you. Even if she doesn't seem wildly passionate each time, don't complain. The very fact that she is involved indicates her unselfish love for you as her husband.

8. Don't forget to enjoy the "afterglow" with your wife! Don't just roll over and go off to sleep. Take time to snuggle with your wife after lovemaking, reminding her of your love and reinforcing the fact that sexual intimacy means more to you than merely satisfying your physical urges. What a gracious blessing from God it is for a husband and wife to fall asleep in each other's loving arms.

DISCUSSION QUESTIONS AND ACTION STEPS
A Passionate Love

Discussion Questions

1. If you are already a believer, do you see God smiling when He looks at you? Why or why not? Read Romans 8:1–4. How does this passage relate to this question?

2. Why do you think we sometimes struggle to think of God's love for us in terms of emotions, that is, that God loves us passionately? See Isaiah 62:5; 65:17–19 and Zephaniah 3:17.

3. How do you think your church's worship might change if more believers grasped the reality of the Lord's passionate love for them?

4. In this chapter we learned that romance involves talking, time, touching, and thoughtful actions. In your own relationship with your wife, which of those expressions of romantic love would you especially like to improve upon? How can you be more intentional in touching your wife's heart and mind before touching her body?

5. Read 1 Corinthians 7:2–5. What does this passage teach us about committing to serve our wives by satisfying them sexually and not merely expecting them to satisfy our needs?

Action Steps

1. Take your wife out to dinner at a place you know she enjoys. Take the initiative in planning the evening—making the reservation, arranging for a babysitter, and so forth. During dinner, tell her of your love for her and of your desire to grow in romancing her. Ask her to tell you some ways you could help her feel special. You might want to jot these down!

2. This week, as much as possible, each evening go to bed at the same time as your wife. In bed, read aloud together a chapter

or two of the Song of Solomon. Ask her what touches her heart from the passages you read. (The rest of this homework assignment is up to you and your wife!)

3. If you and your wife have been experiencing sexual difficulties, plan a time this week when you can calmly and compassionately talk about it. Ask her questions that convey your love and your commitment to seeking solutions to your difficulties. Avoid expressions of frustration or self-defensiveness as you speak to your wife about these sensitive issues. (You might want to purchase a copy of *Intended for Pleasure* by Dr. Ed Wheat and his wife, Gaye Wheat, then read those sections with your wife that deal most directly with the struggles you are facing as a couple. See the Sources section at the back of this book).

10

A Praying Love

Jesus and eleven of His apostles descended the stairs from the Upper Room and headed through the darkened streets of Jerusalem, across the gully to the east of Jerusalem, on their way to the Garden of Gethsemane. This was a night to be forever remembered. This was the night before the cross. This was the night of Jesus' passion.

Somewhere along that moonlit walk, maybe as the group was passing by the temple complex, Jesus paused to pour out His heart to His heavenly Father. As Jews customarily did, Jesus prayed aloud. Surely the cavesdropping apostles found some reassurance for their confused hearts as Jesus lifted His eyes, hands, and voice toward heaven.

As they listened, the apostles may have realized that Jesus was praying not only for them but also for other generations who would become His followers through the disciples' ministry. In the years that followed, as the Holy Spirit reminded them of the events of that night before the cross, I wonder if thoughts of the loving concern Jesus demonstrated in this prayer warmed their hearts.

Christ Demonstrated a Praying Love for His Church

Jesus revealed His heart that night. Though He knew His humiliating and horrifying execution on that Roman cross was only hours away, He showed concerned for His chosen people. In His prayer

Jesus revealed that His followers—that we—were on His heart. In John 17 Jesus demonstrated His tender passion for us, His bride, with a praying love.

In this prayer, often referred to as the High Priestly Prayer, Jesus clearly focused His love, not on the world in general but on those whom the Father had given Him—those whom He would redeem on the cross the next morning. John 17:9 quotes Jesus: "I pray for them. I am not praying for the world, but for those you have given me, for they are yours."

We could legitimately say that Jesus was praying for His soon-to-be-redeemed bride, the church. In this passionately loving prayer, Jesus prays for His bride's protection, especially from "the evil one" (John 17:11 and 15). He prays that His bride would "have the full measure of my joy" (v. 13).

Jesus reveals His love when He says to His heavenly Father, "Sanctify them by the truth; your word is truth" (v. 17). He reveals His concern when he asks that the church "may be one as we are one; I in them and you in me. May they be brought to complete unity" (vv. 22–23). He reveals His affection for His bride when He requests, "Father, I want those you have given me to be with me where I am, and to see my glory" (v. 24).

Jesus even asks that the love the Father has for Him may be in us (v. 26). Yes, in those hours before His rapidly approaching crucifixion, Jesus demonstrates His unquestionable love by pouring out His heart for His church.

Jesus Calls Us to Demonstrate a Praying Love for Our Wives

And, once again, He is our Model for loving our wives. Bob Lepine writes, "If a husband will love and serve his wife as Christ loves His church, then the intercessory prayer of Christ in John 17 becomes a model for how a priestly husband can intercede on behalf of his wife."[1]

I heartily agree. But, like many Christian men, for too many years my commitment to pray *for* my wife and *with* my wife was more theoretical than actual. For how many years was my time alone with my wife before God's throne almost nonexistent. Some prayers of thanks for the food at mealtimes and some "let's-wrap-up-family-

devotions" prayers with the kids were about the only p
honestly claim as my own.

Then I received some biblical instruction regarding *why* I should
pray with my wife, *what* I should pray, and *how* I should pray. And
that, among other factors, served as a catalyst to move me beyond
"Thanks for the food, Lord."

I wonder how many men would confess, "Actually, I avoid praying with my wife because I just don't know how." Let's look at some
principles that may help.

Why Should We Pray with Our Wives?

*First, prayer with our wives teaches us humility and opens our hearts to
God's grace.* We desperately need God's grace in our own lives as men
and in our marriages, don't we? Our attempts to make life work, to
make our marriages work—on our own—are futile and foolish. So,
what gets the attention of our grace-dispensing God?

Humility. Both Peter (in 1 Peter 5:5) and James (in 4:6) echo
Proverbs 3:34, when they write, "God opposes the proud but gives
grace to the humble." C. J. Mahaney writes, "God is decisively
drawn to humility. The person who is humble is the one who draws
God's attention, and in this sense, drawing His attention means also
attracting His grace–His unmerited kindness."[2] We need that. We
need God's grace.

It's so hard to be proud in God's presence, isn't it? How can we
be? The very act of praying is a way of confessing, "You are God and
I am not. You are the One in control, not I. You are the One who
knows how to solve the problems I face in life, not I. You are the One
who has both the power and the authority to effect the changes I so
desperately need in my life and marriage, not I."

Coming into the throne room of the Sovereign of the Universe is
humbling work, and that is good and right. Nineteenth century pastor E. M. Bounds wrote, "Prayer is humbling work. It abases intellect
and pride, crucifies vainglory, and signs our spiritual bankruptcy, and
all these are hard for flesh and blood to bear."[3]

The very act of praying does humble us. And humility draws the
grace of God that we so greatly need.

Second, prayer with our wives can help us develop an increased intimacy with God. To be honest, I have often treated prayer as a means of presenting God with a grocery list of my needs and desires. But prayer should be—and can be—so much more. When I pray with my wife, I can pursue a deeper intimacy with the Lord myself while encouraging my wife to develop her own closeness with the Lord at the same time.

- As we devote time and attention to the Lord, our bond of affection with Him grows.

- As we reflect back to Him in prayer what we adore about Him—His attributes of greatness and grace—our hearts grow warmer.

- As we recall in His presence what we appreciate about Him—the many acts of kindness and forgiveness He has shown us—our grateful affections increase.

Praying with my wife promotes an increased intimacy with the Lord who bought us. Let's experience with our wives the benefit promised in James: "Come near to God and he will come near to you" (4:8).

Third, prayer with our wives strengthens our marriage bond. As we pray with our wives, we hear their hearts, gaining insights into their desires, concerns, and fears in a way that might not be revealed as freely in any other venue. A husband can connect with his wife in a "soulish" way as he listens to her pour out her heart before her heavenly Father. The husband, in turn then, praying for her concerns, confirms his unity with her. He reminds her of his own confidence in God's commitment to her welfare. Husband and wife develop an intimacy in prayer that cannot be matched in any other way. Praying together is not merely the uniting of two bodies; it is the uniting of two souls—true spiritual intimacy.

Our wives may feel that intimacy more strongly than we suspect. My wife caught me completely off guard one morning after our time of prayer together. After the final amen, while we were still holding hands (as we usually do when we pray together), she looked at me and said, "I desire you physically after we pray more than at any other time."

After the initial shock wore off, I think I smiled and a dramatic pastoral voice, "Let us pray!" But seriously, implying that in praying together she felt a spiritual intimacy with me that sought expression in physical intimacy. Praying together can be that powerful.

When a husband, in his wife's hearing, takes her concerns before the throne of the King of the Universe, he assures her he lovingly desires her protection from danger and her growth in grace. Then her trust in him grows, not only as she hears him pray with her but also as he lovingly reminds her he's praying for her throughout his day.

Stormie Omartian writes, "I know that one thing every woman wants to hear, the thing that will make her feel more loved than anything else, is 'I'm praying for you today.'"[4]

Based on a 1989-1990 Gallup/*Psychology Today* two-part study titled *Love and Marriage*, well-known sociologist and author Andrew M. Greeley wrote a nonfiction book, *Faithful Attraction*. He comments on the positive effects of husbands and wives praying together. "Whether they pray often together or not is a very powerful correlate of marital happiness, the most powerful we have yet discovered," he writes. "Prayer...is a much more powerful predictor of marital satisfaction than frequency of sexual intercourse—though the combination of sex and prayer correlates with very, very high levels of marital fulfillment."[5]

A couple in the entertainment industry, husband and wife authors SQuire Rushnell and Louise DuArt, were so moved by the transforming power of prayer in their own marriage, that they wrote *Couples Who Pray: The Most Intimate Act Between a Man and a Woman*. Included in their book is a 40-day prayer challenge and testimonials from celebrity couples whose marriages benefited greatly from praying together. As part of their research, they asked Byron Johnson, head of Baylor University's Institute for Studies of Religion, to reanalyze the *Love and Marriage* study. Johnson's colleague in preparing the analysis, sociology professor Jerry Park, came to this conclusion: "People who pray with their spouses a lot, compared to people who pray with their spouses sometimes, find that their lives and marriages improve, often with astonishing results."[6]

Here are a few of those results:[7]

Area of marriage	Couples praying together sometimes	Couples praying together a lot
Say "marriage is happy"	60%	78%
Satisfaction with sex life ("a great deal" or "a very great deal")	67%	82%
Confidence in stability of marriage	76%	92%

These results bear out the teaching of Scripture. We can apply the wisdom of Ecclesiastes 4:12 to the practice of praying to God as a husband-wife team: "A cord of three strands is not quickly broken." How difficult it is to break the bond when husband and wife intertwine their hearts with the Lord through prayer! Couples that pray together stay together.

Fourth, prayer with our wives gives us the opportunity to seek the Lord's help in our marriages, our families, and our daily lives. How often have we failed to find solutions to our problems and resorted to prayer only in desperation? Pastor and author Alistair Begg candidly observes:

> It is troubling when husbands and wives don't pray together. They try nearly everything else—reading books, consulting counselors, creating strategies to work through a difficult situation. Yet prayer seems to be the final resort instead of the first option. If they are willing to go to counselors, pas-

tors, and books for solutions, how much better it would be to consult the One who created us, who knows us better than we know ourselves, and who loves us enough to die for us.[8]

Our Lord wants us to come to Him with the concerns of our hearts and the problems in our lives. He paid an inestimably high price—the precious blood of His much-loved Son—to give us this access to His throne room. Let's faithfully commit to heed the call of Hebrews 4:16: "Let us then approach the throne of grace with confidence, so that we may receive mercy and find grace to help us in our time of need."

What Should We Pray for Our Wives?

I know many men struggle with praying for their wives. Sometimes we don't know what to say in our prayers. Maybe a good place to start is to go to our Savior, repeating this request from His first disciples, "Lord, teach us to pray" (Luke 11:1).

He has promised to guide us. And there are several rich mines we can explore to gain insight into what we should be praying for our wives:

1. *The Scriptures themselves.* Let's pay attention to many of the prayers found in the Psalms. Might some of these contain gems that we can transform into prayers for our wives? How about the prayers of Paul for the church? Look at Ephesians 1:15–23 and 3:14–21 for ideas we might turn into prayers for our wives. For example, what might happen in our wives' hearts when they hear us pray these words from Ephesians 1:17, "I keep asking that the God of our Lord Jesus Christ, the glorious Father, may give you the Spirit of wisdom and revelation, so that you may know him better"? That's a prayer request with some substance!

2. *Thoughtful observations of their lives.* Most of us could grow in the daily practice of studying our wives. How is she spending her time? What are the concerns she talks about? What emotions have you been observing in her life of late? Let's not ignore these. Our wives

would no doubt be pleasantly surprised to hear us tenderly praying for them in specific ways arising from our own observations of their lives and from listening to their hearts.

3. *Asking our wives!* We would have no problem knowing how to pray for our wives if we simply asked on a regular basis, "Honey, how can I be praying for you today?" My hunch is that after getting over the novelty of the question, our wives will begin anticipating it, and have some prayer requests ready for us.

Here are some specific areas of prayer for your wife and marriage that I've gleaned from my wife, other writers, and my own observations:

- Most importantly, pray for yourself. Pray that you would continually grow to be the man God has directed you to be as a loving leader to your wife and family.

- Pray for your wife's spiritual growth and perseverance: her reading, understanding and application of God's Word; her sensitivity to sin; her daily embracing of the gospel; and her treasuring of Christ above all else.

- Ask the Lord to protect your wife physically, emotionally, doctrinally and spiritually. John Piper says, "Fight for them in prayer against the devil and the world and the flesh. Pray the prayers of the Bible for them. Don't grow weary. God hears and answers prayer for our wives and children."[9]

- Ask the Lord, on your wife's behalf, to enable her to be a wife and mother who pleases Him.

- Pray that there might be a sweet unity in her relationships with extended family on both her side and yours.

- Pray for godly female friends for your wife who would encourage her in her daily walk with the Lord. In particular, ask the Lord to provide for your wife a godly older woman (as described in Titus 2:3–5) who would nurture your wife through her own example and counsel. Or, if your wife is already of grandmotherly age, pray that she might be a "Titus 2 woman" to younger women.

- Ask God to minister to your wife in the areas of her concerns, struggles, and fears, reminding her, by His Spirit, of God's promises and His sovereign, loving, watchful care over her life.

- Pray for her ministries, that she would know the joy of being a useful instrument in His hand, using the gifts, passions, and opportunities the Spirit has put into her life.

How Should We Pray for Our Wives?

Simply stated, we should have both scheduled and spontaneous times of prayer with our wives. Let's be honest, men. If we don't schedule a time and place to pray with our wives, it probably isn't going to happen. Life is busy, and it's easy to get caught up in the tyranny of the urgent or with distractions and lose sight of the value and discipline of praying with our wives.

A scheduled time. Talk to your wife about what might be the best time for the two of you to spend time together on a regular basis to read God's Word and pray. For those with younger children, the best time may be after the kids are in bed at night. Of course, that will require you, as parents, to make sure the children have a designated bedtime! It will also require avoiding the TV, computer, or other distractions until you have had this precious time with your wife.

Those who do not have children at home may find more flexibility in scheduling a time alone as husband and wife in the presence of the Lord. Since we've become empty nesters, my wife and I have found that we can get together for a devotional time at the breakfast table about five mornings each week. Of course this takes discipline. Realizing that we want to spend this time together requires setting the alarm clock to allow opportunity to read and pray together without starting our day feeling rushed.

A scheduled place. In addition to establishing a time to pray together, I encourage you to establish a place. Although it might work for some couples to have their regular prayer time in bed, I fear many of us would find ourselves falling asleep before our conversation with the Lord is complete. Sitting on a couch or at a table might work better. Others kneel beside their bed together as they pray. Agree with your wife on a place to pray together.

Develop helpful habits in your prayer time with your wife. My wife and I find it beneficial to pray briefly for the Spirit's work in our minds and hearts; then we read together for a while, discussing what we are learning in our reading and what is encouraging or convicting to us. Then, having our hearts primed in this way, we pray again, this time a bit longer, sharing with the Lord our words of praise, thankfulness, confession, and requests.

These are our suggestions. Discuss with your wife what might be helpful for both of you to make this time of prayer together a loving gift to each other.

Unscheduled spontaneity. In addition to these scheduled prayer times, a Christlike husband will also seize spontaneous opportunities to pray with and for his wife. Does your wife seem overwhelmed with her workload or with caring for the children? Why not hold her close and ask the Lord to give her strength and rest? (Then give her a hand!) Does she seem worried? Take her hand and pray that the Spirit will assure her of the Lord's persistent love for her and control over the events of life. Is she convicted about some sin? Stop and lead her to the God who forgives by His grace. You get the idea. Lovingly pay attention to your wife. Learn to "read" her. Then, learn to "lead" her to the throne room of our Sovereign Father.

Hindrances to Praying with Our Wives

Feeling brave? Ask some of your Christian buddies how many of them pray regularly with their wives. My hunch is that you will find that those who do are in the minority—a small minority. If we want to grow in reflecting Christ's praying love, it may be wise for us to evaluate honestly the most common hindrances to praying with our wives.

Busyness

This is no doubt the most common excuse for not praying with our wives. "Our lives are just so hectic," we say. "I've got a demanding job. It seems as though we're always running the kids to practices, games, and recitals. There are house projects. And we try to volunteer at our church. We are constantly living in high gear!"

Life *is* busy. But we need to take time out to evaluate our game plan. Why do we do what we do? What really matters for eternity? Are we sacrificing the essential for the optional? Some optional activities would not be difficult to eliminate or at least reduce. Art Hunt, author of *Praying with the One You Love*, relates this conversation he had with a couple who thought they were too busy to pray: "'So you two were busy and didn't pray. May I ask if you watched any TV together?' They looked at each other and smiled. 'I see your point,' the wife said with a grin."[10] Do you relate to that story? We could substitute the phrase "watched any TV" with "surfed the web" or "read the newspaper."

Other activities that keep us from taking time to pray may not be as easy to excise from our lives, but they should be evaluated. For example, many families are so consumed with sports that nearly everything else takes second or third place. While participation in sports can have benefits, what do we sacrifice in the process? Do these activities limit your "free time" so much that you and your wife can't find time to seek the Lord together? If we truly see the value and benefits of praying as a couple, we'll fight against using the excuse, *We're just too busy to pray.*

Fear

A less-easy-to-talk-about reason for not praying as a couple is that of fear. Men don't readily talk about their fears, but we have them. I wonder how many men don't pray with their wives because they are afraid of revealing their lack of spiritual maturity. Better to avoid that situation altogether, they may think.

Men, as long as we avoid facing this lack of prayer in our marriages, we will perpetuate the spiritual anemia that comes from prayerlessness. The future doesn't have to look like the past. The Lord can give us strength to face this current lack. Ask the Lord's strength. Talk to your wife about your growing conviction that you should pray together. Then get started! Even if your first attempts at praying with your wife are comparatively brief and awkward, they are a beginning. Build on them. Don't abandon your desire to exercise your faith muscles. Day-by-day, week-by-week, your faith will grow and your ministry of praying with your wife and for your wife will strengthen and enrich your marriage.

Pride

Related to the hindrance of fear is pride. As we've already seen, prayer is humbling work. Might it be pride that is keeping us from praying with our wives? Any attitudes of superiority and self-justification in our lives will hinder our praying with our wives.

In our hearts, we realize that if we go before the King with our wives, those sinful facades will be stripped away. Pride actually invites the Lord's opposition to our foolish attempts to make life work on our own (James 4:6). So instead of hanging onto that pride, why not humble ourselves so we can pray freely with our wives and experience God's grace?

Could this be one of the implications of Peter's counsel in 1 Peter 3:7? "Husbands, in the same way be considerate as you live with your wives, and treat them with respect [literally, grant them honor] as the weaker partner and as heirs with you of the gracious gift of life, so that nothing will hinder your prayers."

Jesus loves us, His bride, and demonstrates His love by praying for us. As we married men seek to mirror Jesus, we, too, will show our wives our love by praying with them and for them. Art Hunt encourages us with this reminder: "What happens when couples pray? Many things, all of them good. Marriages are enriched—some are literally transformed! Couples who share a prayer life together discover that the time, commitment, energy, and risk are all very worthwhile. Prayer definitely makes a difference!"[11]

DISCUSSION QUESTIONS AND ACTION STEPS
A Praying Love

Discussion Questions

1. Read John 17:6–26. What evidences of Jesus' love for us can you find in His prayer?

2. Read Hebrews 7:23–25 and 1 John 2:1. These passages teach us that Jesus faithfully and constantly intercedes for us before the throne of His Father. How does this ongoing ministry of Jesus affect your view of Him and His dedication to you? How might this truth affect your daily life?

3. Other than at meal times, when do you pray with your wife? What are some of your *heart issues* that keep you from praying with your wife? What *heart changes* will you ask God to do in your life so you can more consistently show your wife a Christlike praying love?

4. What *lifestyle and schedule choices* have you made that hinder you from having regular prayer times with your wife? What changes do you feel the Holy Spirit is calling you to make so you can be more faithful in praying with your wife? Be specific.

Action Steps

1. Talk to your wife this week about what the Lord has been teaching you about your role in loving her with a praying love. Tell her you desire to pray with her regularly. Ask her to suggest the best time for her—first thing in the morning? Before going off to work? Bedtime? Then get started!

2. Before leaving for work each day this week, ask your wife how you can be praying for her throughout the day. Then, taking her hand or holding her close, pray aloud for her personally and about her concerns. Ask God's gracious blessing upon her. Then give her a kiss. Make this morning routine a loving habit.

3. The next time your wife expresses confusion or frustration about a decision or incident in her life, don't ignore her. Don't try to offer quick-fix advice. Instead, say something like this: "Honey, I can hear your concern (frustration). I care about what you're feeling. Let's take that concern to the Lord right now." Then, taking her hand or holding her close, pray about that issue on her heart, asking for the Lord's grace, wisdom, and direction. Ask her if she wants to pray, too. Keep doing this until it becomes a loving pattern of how you minister to your wife with a praying love in times of concern, confusion, or frustration.

11

A Purifying
Love

A "purifying" love? What does that mean? It's probably safe to assume that few husbands have had much teaching on how to show love to their wives in a purifying way. Yet, Ephesians 5:26–27 teaches that one of the demonstrations of Christ's love for His bride is His commitment "to make her holy, cleansing her by the washing with water through the word, and to present her to himself as a radiant church, without stain or wrinkle or any other blemish, but holy and blameless."

If we husbands are to love our wives "as Christ loved the church," how do these verses play out in our own marriages? Am I really supposed to be responsible in some measure for my wife's spiritual health and growth?

Earlier in my marriage to Gladine, I became frustrated with certain attitudes and behaviors I thought I detected in my wife. I have to confess that I had a less-than-honorable attitude about what I perceived as her spiritual faults and shortcomings. I remember thinking, "Why doesn't she just change? What's wrong with her? Why can't she act in a more spiritually mature way?"

Then the Lord began to convict *me* for *my* sinful attitudes. It was as if the Holy Spirit asked me, "Who do you think I ordained to be your wife's primary discipler?" That concept—that I am my wife's primary discipler—began to take root in my conscience. Slowly and awkwardly, I began to see these concerns not merely as hers but mine. The Holy Spirit wanted to use me as an agent—maybe even the primary agent—in His sovereign and gracious hand as He lovingly continued His process of conforming my precious wife to the image of Christ. He wanted me to love my wife with a purifying love.

My hunch is that this subject could polarize readers. Let's be candid. Some guys seem to have a proud bent to control (or at least try to control) their wives, and they may assume this chapter will affirm their self-proclaimed spiritual superiority in the home. At the other end of the spectrum, other men will have a knee-jerk reaction to our even addressing such a topic in the twenty-first century: What right does a man have to tell his wife how to live the Christian life?

But let's go back to what we know about our Model, The Perfect Husband, Jesus Christ. Let's think through how He loves His bride, the church, in a purifying way.

Christ's Goal for His Bride

Christ explicitly loves His bride, seeking to make her spiritually beautiful. He is so committed to this goal that He was willing to sacrifice His own life on a Roman cross to accomplish it: "Christ loved the church and gave himself up for her, *to make her holy*" (Ephesians 5:25–26, emphasis added). Using first-century wedding terminology, the Apostle Paul writes with the Ultimate Wedding Day in view—the wedding of Christ, the Lamb, and His bride, the church. (For more details about the Great Wedding Day, see Revelation 19:7–9 and 21:2). It's as if Christ Himself is looking forward to that Great Wedding and is passionately and persistently preparing His bride for that glorious day. Jesus wants to present His bride "to himself as a radiant church, without stain or wrinkle or any other blemish, but holy and blameless" (Ephesians 5:27).

Understanding first-century Jewish wedding customs can help us better grasp the imagery of Ephesians 5. New Testament scholar Dr. Harold Hoehner explains, "In Jewish customs at the time of betrothal the young man would present his bride-to-be with a gift and say to her, 'Behold, you are consecrated to me, you are betrothed to me; behold, you are a wife unto me.' With this spoken word they would be betrothed and then married about a year later. Just before the wedding she was bathed, symbolizing the cleansing that would set her apart to her husband."[1]

In Ephesians 5 Paul uses this just-before-the-wedding bath to picture Christ's purifying love for His bride, the church. It symbolizes her spiritual cleansing from the bitter sin that hinders her relationship with Him, a relationship intended to be enjoyably sweet. Christ keeps in view that day when the church will be "without stain or wrinkle or any other blemish, but holy and blameless" (v. 27), indeed, "a bride beautifully dressed for her husband" (Revelation 21:2). This Husband, who committed Himself to His bride with a purifying love, accomplishes His glorious goal by two primary means, by cleansing her and by feeding her.

Christ Loves His Bride by Cleansing Her

The word *cleansing* in Ephesians 5:26 pictures the corrective aspect of our transformation—cleansing us from the defilement of our sin. He does this by "the washing with water through the word." The terminology Paul uses here refers to a message, something spoken.[2] He is likely writing about the gospel message of God's grace that is preached to us, drawing us *away* from our addiction to our sin and *toward* a life of treasuring Christ and living for Him instead.

Christ persistently and progressively demonstrates His love for us as His Holy Spirit takes the gospel message and scrubs our lives, washing away whatever sins keep us from full-hearted devotion to our glorious Husband. How kind of Him! How loving!

Christ Loves His Bride by Feeding Her

But Christ also *feeds* His bride (Ephesians 5:29). We often refer to this formative side of the life-transformation coin as our sanctification. Christ is constantly showing His love for us by giving us "everything we need for life and godliness" (2 Peter 1:3). Our Perfect Husband is committed to loving us by being intimately and continuously involved in our lives, providing everything we need—the Holy Spirit, His precious Word, pastors and teachers, Christian friends, and even suffering. He offers it all to encourage our spiritual growth and maturity. He wants us to become His beautiful bride.

He never loses sight of the goal of that wonderful wedding day and the inexpressible bliss that will follow for an eternity. He has proven His commitment to love us in this purifying way by "giving himself up" for us.

How Can We Love Our Wives with a Purifying Love?

Men, in order to "love our wives as Christ loves the church," we bear a unique responsibility for their spiritual health and growth.

Our Lord commissioned us to be the "primary disciplers" of our wives. So it would be wise for us to consider seriously how we might accomplish this glorious mission.

By the Influence of a Christlike Example

Let's start with the positive. How can we be tools in the Lord's hand to lead our wives toward spiritual maturity? Let's not miss the obvious. Our own example, how we live the Christian life day by day—even without a word—can and does have a powerful influence on our wives (and children) for good or for bad. Realizing this responsibility should sober us.

If I were to say to my wife, "Follow me" and she accepted my invitation, would she be closer to Christ or further away from Him?

The apostle Paul told the Corinthian believers, "Follow my example, as I follow the example of Christ" (1 Corinthians 11:1). That should be the humble, heart-felt cry of each married man to his wife and family.

But how consistently are we following Christ? 1 John 2:5–6 says, "This is how we know we are in him: Whoever claims to live in him must walk as Jesus did." What happens when my wife watches me and sees the value I put on God and His glory, the choices I make in life, how I respond to the influences of this world, and how I treat people? Does she see a reflection of Christ? Am I giving my wife a model of Christlikeness she can follow in her own quest for spiritual health and maturity?[3]

Realizing the importance of pursuing Christlikeness, not only for the sake of my own soul but also for my wife's, I must devote myself to a life of following Him and reflecting His character as I live everyday life as a married man. By God's grace, I need to be a consistent example of what the Lord wants my wife to become.

By Leading Planned Teaching Times with Her

I can almost hear the response of some men right now. "Whoa! I'm no teacher! I don't think anyone should expect me to be teaching the Bible to my wife. She probably knows more about the Bible than I do anyway!"

Guys, I've been married for more than 30 years. I've served as a pastor for most of that time. And I can assure you from what I've heard from my own wife and numerous women in our church over the years that *married women hunger for their husbands to be spiritual leaders in the home.* In fact, I would venture to say that this is the most common complaint I've heard from women in marriage counseling sessions.

It's humbling to admit this was true in my own marriage. For years I was busy caring for the spiritual needs of other people in our congregation while neglecting the spiritual needs of my own wife. And I hurt her deeply.

There were times she would say, "All I want for my birthday this year is for you to take time to lead me spiritually. Let's read God's Word together. Let's pray together. That's all I want."

To my shame, I was not reflecting Christ. I was not loving my wife in a purifying way. So the Lord graciously began to work me over, moving me to repent and to gladly commit to being personally involved with my wife as her primary spiritual leader.

Want to join me in this pursuit?

An obvious place for any married man feeling inadequate in this area is to humble himself before God and ask for help. Maybe say something to Him like this: "Lord, I know you want me to love my wife with a purifying love, just like you love Your bride, the church, washing her through the Word. I know you want me to feed her spiritually. I'm willing to try, Lord, but I need your help. Please help me."

Want some good news? Remember: God says He gives grace to the humble. As you humble yourself before Him, watch how He will begin to use you in your wife's spiritual growth.

Here's a simple but significant way to approach your wife about this: Talk to her. Confess your shortcomings as a spiritual leader thus far in your marriage. Let her know you want to change. Ask for her prayer support and loving encouragement. Together select a workable time to read God's Word together. As I mentioned earlier, for us it's at the breakfast table five days per week. You and your wife may find another time, frequency, and place more suitable.

If you truthfully feel inadequate to teach your wife from the Bible, do what you can at this time and commit to grow. You may want to find a devotional book for couples and simply read it aloud to her during your devotional time together. Some books include discussion questions that can help you lead your wife in applying what you've just read together.

My wife and I often pray briefly before we read from a daily devotional or directly from a passage in the Bible, asking God to lead us to understand and apply what He wants us to learn. Then, we often pray after our reading, seeking God's blessing and guidance on the day ahead. It's not complicated, but it's a great way to start living out God's commission to disciple your wife. Not only does this please the Lord, but also your wife will bless you for blessing her this way!

By Spontaneously Applying God's Word in Daily Situations

As we become more immersed in God's Word, we more readily see ways to assist our wives in applying its truths to various situations we encounter. Without becoming "preachy," we can lovingly remind our wives of the hope and help we find in God's precious Word.

In decision making, with the Bible as our standard, we can encourage our wives' growth in grace by helping them think through various options before them.

In rearing the children together, we can lead our wives in setting biblical priorities and boundaries as parents, and this, too, can be a significant boost to spiritual growth.

In times of trials, we can take our wives to the hope we find in the rock of God's revelation that can strengthen their faith.

In times when they are wounded by others or feeling disappointment, discouragement, and even depression, we can come alongside our wives with the balm of God's Word and can remind them of His absolutely reliable love.

Much of our wives' spiritual growth will happen during these spontaneous opportunities the Lord brings us for showing them how valuable and practical His Word is for living life and growing in grace.

By Helping Her Learn God's Truths from Others

Another way to encourage your wife's spiritual growth is to take loving initiative in providing other ways for her to grow spiritually. Though we touched on this earlier we need to consider it again here.

1. *Commit to being a vital part of your local body of believers.* How involved are you—individually and as a couple—in a Bible-teaching church? Does your church have Bible studies for women? Encourage her to participate, volunteering to watch the children, if possible, so she can attend. Take the initiative (that's what leaders do!) in exploring the possibilities of you and your wife getting involved in a small group Bible study, an adult Christian education class at your church, or a weekend marriage retreat.

2. *Help her connect with God personally.* Have you heard her say that she finds it hard to find quiet time to read the Bible on her own? What could you do to help in that situation? Why not volunteer to watch the kids for a while, encouraging her to find a quiet corner of the house to get alone with God?

3. *Encourage time to read spiritually uplifting books.* If she likes to read, she may have a list she's been waiting to get time for. Facilitate that time for her. If she needs book suggestions, ask your pastor or another godly person in the church what books he or she might recommend that you buy or borrow for your wife.

4. *Fill your home (and car) with God-centered music.* The melodies and biblical lyrics of Christian music can take up residence in her heart and mind and help build her up in her faith. What can you do to encourage her in this area?

You're getting the picture, aren't you? God's Word is a powerful tool in His sovereign hands to shape our own lives—and our wives'. Remember what 2 Timothy 3:16 says? "All Scripture is God-breathed and is useful for teaching, rebuking, correcting and training in righteousness." Let's look for ways to help our wives encounter the powerful Word of God, prayerfully desiring to see them grow more and more spiritually mature as a result.

By Helping Her Deal with Sin in Her Life

Why do I find this ministry of helping my wife deal with sin in her life to be one of the most intimidating? Do I fear her rejection? Do I fear having my own sin exposed in the process? Yet, my commission as a husband still stands: to "love my wife as Christ loved the church and gave himself up for her, to make her holy, cleansing her by the washing with water through the word."[4]

What is my role in cleansing my wife? Let's use Galatians 6:1 as home base in exploring this scary but significant means of serving our wives with a purifying love: "Brothers, if someone is caught in a sin, you who are spiritual should restore him gently. But watch yourself, or you also may be tempted."

How might this verse apply when a husband senses some sinful attitude or action may have cropped up in his wife's life? What guidelines can we derive from this God-inspired verse for becoming agents of the Holy Spirit in washing sin from our wives' lives?

- *A humble approach.* Why did Paul warn would-be restorers to watch themselves? Because we are all prone to sin and susceptible to temptation. If the Lord is going to use a husband in helping the wife deal with sin in her life, there is no place for proud finger pointing. This is not a "gotcha" event, as author David Harvey puts it.[5] Banish proud thoughts and comments such as, "I can't believe you did that!"

  Guys, each of us needs to acknowledge that he's not the only one who married a sinner. So did his wife! Before I attempt eye surgery on the speck in my wife's eye, am I humbly acknowledging the plank in my own eye, seeking to extricate it by God's grace? (Matthew 7:1–5) It's a probing question I don't ask myself often enough.

  Would my wife see Christ-honoring humility in my life if I approach her with an offer to help her with sin in hers? Or would she find a smug, superior attitude, causing her to draw away, calling me a hypocrite?

- *An honest approach.* In Galatians 6:1, sin is clearly seen as sin. Paul doesn't minimize it as a mistake or a bad decision. Seeing sins (whether our own or our wife's) for what they are—bitter offenses against a holy, gracious God that keep us from glorifying Him and enjoying Him—makes grace and forgiveness all the more sweet. When we minimize sin, we also minimize God's grace. Dave Harvey explains, "By far the greatest benefit of acknowledging our sinfulness is that it makes Christ and his work precious to us....Only sinners need a Savior."[6]

As we deal with sin in our marriages, we need to resist the temptation to look for a quick fix so we can get on with life. Let's be honest, men. How many times have we addressed issues with our wives in a superficial way, seeking merely to patch things up between the two of us so we no longer have to live with the hassle of the rift in our relationship?

Where is God in all this? Where is sin? If my wife has sinned, the real issue is that she has offended her Lord. That's what sin is: an offense against God. The healing needed is a soul healing. A healing of the rift between (in this case) my wife and her Lord. As I lead her humbly, but honestly in dealing with the sin, the Holy Spirit can do His gracious work of applying gospel-sweet forgiveness to her soul.

- *A hopeful approach.* There's a word in Galatians 6:1 that is marinated in hope. It's the word "restore." Our motivation is restoration, not condemnation. I suspect some of us who have been married more than a few weeks can recall times when we harshly pointed out sin in our wives with sarcastic remarks devoid of hope: "You'll never change! You'll always be a _____!" Those damaging, devastating words, motivated by a spiteful anger, seek to justify our own sin by making hers look worse. They're not motivated by a purifying love that seeks our wives' ultimate spiritual beauty.

The goal of the spiritual restorer of Galatians 6:1 is always restoration. The idea behind the word "restore" is "to make useful again." The spiritual husband wants his wife to be useful to the Master again (2 Timothy 2:20–21), knowing the joy of being an instrument in His hand. So this means speaking words of hope into his wife's soul as he humbly and honestly deals with the sin.

Men, in humility we can point our wives to the Savior, reassuring them that "there is now no condemnation for those who are in Christ Jesus" (Romans 8:1). God has not condemned us. Why would we condemn our wives? In Christ we can be forgiven and restored to a place of usefulness for His glory. Tears of repentance and confession can lead to smiles of forgiveness and restoration.

• *A humane approach.* When we hear the word *humane*, pictures of gentleness and compassion may come to mind. Would those be the words that come to my wife's mind when she recalls how I deal with her sin: *gentle* and *compassionate*? Yet Galatians 6:1 says those who wield the scalpel of God's Word, attempting to do soul surgery to rid others of the cancers of sin, must do so gently. There is no reason to hack away at anyone's soul, let alone our beloved wives'.

David Harvey sees kindness as essential. "Kindness says to our spouse, 'I know you are a sinner like me, and you will sin against me, just like I sin against you. But I refuse to live defensively with you. I'm going to live leaning in your direction with a merciful posture that your sin and weakness cannot erase.'"[7]

Guys, any time we seek to deal with sin in our wives, we must carry the aroma of our gentle and compassionate Savior into surgery.

The words of author and radio speaker Bob Lepine should serve as a reminder when we are tempted to deal harshly with our wives' offenses: "Most wives don't need a constant reminder of their own sin, especially from their husbands. They are painfully aware of their shortcomings and their failures. Instead, they need to be reminded of God's forgiveness when they stumble. They need to hear again that his mercies are new every morning. They long for encouragement."[8]

By Keeping the Goal in Sight

The Perfect Husband, Jesus Christ, has a glorious goal in loving His bride with a purifying love: He wants "to present her to himself as a radiant church, without stain or wrinkle or any other blemish" (Ephesians 5:27). Though we are an imperfect bride this side of heaven, He never takes His eyes off that glorious day when we will be perfect. He continues to be lovingly involved in our lives, washing away our stains and smoothing out our wrinkles.

Though imperfect reflectors of the Perfect Husband, you and I should love our wives the best we can with a purifying love, never losing sight of the goal—helping them become more like Christ.

Ultimately, serving my wife by helping her deal with sin in her life is not merely about making our marriage relationship better (though that's a wonderful result!). It's about helping my wife see the bitterness of sin so that she might experience the sweetness of Christ.[9] It's about pointing her toward the Son so she might enjoy His beauty and bask in the sunshine of His grace.

Ultimately, my desire must be to see her conformed to the image of Christ Himself (2 Corinthians 3:18), not to some image of my own making. On that great day, by God's amazing grace, my beautiful wife will glow with the reflection of the unsurpassable beauty of Christ.

DISCUSSION QUESTIONS AND ACTION STEPS
A Purifying Love

Discussion Questions

1. What is the primary "tool" in the Lord's hand as He loves us with a purifying love, cleansing us and forming us to become the beautiful bride pictured in Revelation 21:1–2? See Ephesians 5:25–27. What light does Titus 2:11–14 shed on Christ's use of the gospel, not only in our initial salvation but also in our ongoing sanctification?

2. How can you personally let the gospel permeate your life so you can steadily grow in Christian maturity? What changes will this require in your current schedule and lifestyle?

3. Who would you say are the three most influential people in your wife's spiritual health and growth? Are you on that short list? If not, what would have to change for you to be your wife's primary discipler?

4. Think about ways in which the example of your daily life influences your wife's spiritual health and progress (both positively and negatively). What changes is the Holy Spirit calling you to make?

5. One of the actions steps from the chapter entitled "A Purposeful Love" was to discuss with your wife a plan for the two of you to have regular times together reading God's Word and praying. How has it been going?

Action Steps

1. Read Galatians 6:1–2 with your wife. Talk about how you, as a couple, can live out those principles in your marriage when either of you sins. Discuss some of the points in this chapter, regarding the need for spiritual correction—the need to be humble, honest, hopeful, and humane. Talk openly about how you have previously dealt with sin in each other's lives. Do you

need to confess times when you've treated each other wrongly and then request forgiveness? Make a commitment to serve each other lovingly in these ways whenever you become aware of sin in each other's lives.

2. Consider reading and discussing together Dave Harvey's book, *When Sinners Say, "I Do."* (See the Sources section at the back of this book.)

3. In what practical ways can you encourage your wife to avail herself of other sources of positive spiritual input in her life? Taking classes at your church? Taking notes during sermons? Being part of a women's group? Reading helpful Christian books? Take the initiative, without being pushy, to encourage your wife in these ways.

12

A Pardoning Love

I was in the middle of my weekly get together with the men in my accountability group when my cell phone buzzed. I took a peek at the caller ID. It was my wife. But since we were praying, I thought I would return the call at the end of our prayer time. When I checked the voice mail a few minutes later, this is what I heard: "Larry, I locked the keys in the car, and I need to leave right away on an emergency call [a friend was in dire need]! Can you come now so I can use your van until the locksmith comes?"

I'm grateful that our home is only a few miles from the restaurant where my accountability group meets, but in those few minutes of driving time, I have to admit that my mind began to review, "How many times over the years has she locked the keys in the car? I never lock the keys in the car!"[1]

Here is an everyday event (well, I hope not every day) that I think many husbands can relate to. Our wives do things that annoy us, irritate us. Things we might label as careless or thoughtless. Things that really bug us.

How are we husbands supposed to respond to those irritating things that our wives do that get under our skin? Raise our voices in anger? Repeatedly remind them of how careless they can be? Give them the "ice man" treatment so they realize how much they have inconvenienced us? Get back at them by doing something we know really bugs them?

All too often, our reactions to those irritations are rather juvenile, aren't they? We may all have embarrassing memories. In calmer moments, we know those little things our wives do that get under our skin are just that: little things. But what about the big offenses, those hurts that are deliberate sins against us? What if a wife purposefully decides to go against her husband's clearly expressed directive as the head of the home, showing him neither respect nor love? Even worse, what if a wife sins against her husband by committing adultery? How is a husband supposed to respond to that kind of heart-crushing pain?

As much as we might wrestle with its application in certain situations, Ephesians 5:25 provides no exceptions, no escape clauses, and no plea bargains, regardless of how severely a husband's feelings may be hurt. Whether we are talking about some minor irritating inconvenience from a thoughtless wife or the life-shaking, covenant-breaking decisions of an adulterous wife, God's call remains the same: "Husbands, love your wives, just as Christ loved the church."

One of the more pronounced applications of Christ's love for His church is that He forgives sins committed against Him by His bride. Christ's love is a pardoning love.

Christ's Pardoning Love for His Church

In Psalm 103:10 King David says that God "does not treat us as our sins deserve or repay us according to our iniquities." Don't you find that encouraging? What a relief! When we stop to think about it, none of us wants what's "fair." None of us wants God's justice—at least not for ourselves. Fairness would require God to punish us for our many sins. No, we don't want fairness. We want mercy and grace. We want the King to pardon us. "To pardon" means "to release a person from punishment; to not exact the penalty for a crime or offense."[2] Again, in the words of King David, to "not treat us as our sins deserve."

Christ's Pardoning Love Is Patient.

We can be so oblivious to the incalculable sins we have committed against the God who made us. Just think about the multitude of crimes you committed against the High King of Heaven in your headlong pursuit of sin before He chased you down with His undeserved, unexpected saving grace. "But God demonstrates his own love for us in this: While we were still sinners, Christ died for us" (Romans 5:8).

Isn't that astonishing? Why didn't He just squash us ungrateful rebels as if we were some repulsive cockroaches contaminating His holy throne room? The self-admitted "chief of sinners," the apostle Paul, apparently wrestled with this mind-boggling, soul-searching question, too.

Led by the Holy Spirit, he explained to his protégé, Timothy, his own astonishing preservation from God's wrath: "Here is a trustworthy saying that deserves full acceptance: Christ Jesus came into the world to save sinners—of whom I am the worst. *But for that very reason I was shown mercy so that in me, the worst of sinners, Christ Jesus might display his unlimited patience as an example for those who would believe on him and receive eternal life*" (1 Timothy 1:15–16, emphasis added).

In *Walking Like Jesus Did*, I write about the way Jesus provided salvation for this "worst of sinners" to display His amazing attribute of patience. "Instead of crushing this murderous persecutor, Jesus tolerated him day after painful day, week after painful week, month after painful month. And then, one day, wonder of wonders, Jesus poured out His mercy and grace on Saul of Tarsus."[3]

Here's my challenge: "Every Christian should look back [as Paul did] at his life before Christ saved him and ask, 'Why didn't the Lord crush me as I was rebelling against Him? Why did He not send me to hell long ago?' If you are a true follower of Jesus Christ, your life serves as a 'canvas' on which Jesus has painted a portrait of His own character—specifically, His attribute of *patience*.[4]

Jesus truly has loved us with a *pardoning love*, not treating us as our sins deserve!

Christ's Pardoning Love Is Forgiving.

What is forgiveness? The dictionary definition of "forgive" is "to give up resentment against an offender, to give up a desire to punish, or to stop being angry with someone."[5]

The Greek word used most commonly in the New Testament for "forgiveness" has the root concept of "letting go" or "giving it up." We can think of forgiveness as "letting go of the desire for vengeance or retaliation." It is a choice or a decision not to hold grudges or to quit trying to get even when someone hurts us or offends us. Isn't this what Jesus has done for us?

Do you remember the biblical story of the woman who washed Jesus' feet with her tears? In many ways, she represents each of us sinners overwhelmed by Jesus' gift of forgiveness. Luke describes the scene this way: "When a woman who had lived a sinful life in that town learned that Jesus was eating at the Pharisee's house, she brought an alabaster jar of perfume, and as she stood behind him at His feet weeping, she began to wet His feet with her tears. Then she wiped them with her hair, kissed them and poured perfume on them" (Luke 7:37–38).

Although this woman was heartbroken over her sin, the religious leaders of Jesus' day continued to look on her with disdain. But how did Jesus treat this passionately repentant woman? "Jesus said to her, 'Your sins are forgiven'" (Luke 7:48).

Amazingly, Jesus forgave even those who were *not* seeking His forgiveness. I illustrate this in *Walking Like Jesus Did*:

> As Jesus was being nailed to the cross, His first public utterance was…'Father, forgive them.' For whom was Jesus asking forgiveness? Jesus was asking the Father to forgive the Jewish leaders—the very people who had twisted His teaching, slandered His character and insisted upon His crucifixion. Jesus was asking the Father also to forgive the Roman soldiers who had so horribly abused him with rods, whips, fists, and the crown of thorns…Jesus was asking the Father to forgive the crowd, gathered and gawking at the foot of the cross. As the jeering spectators were spewing out words of hatred and mockery, Jesus was at that very time asking His heavenly Father to forgive them.[6]

Jesus forgave those who hurt Him severely! Our forgiveness cost Him dearly. He didn't ignore our offenses. Jesus never said, "Oh well, what are you going to do? I guess boys will be boys. Okay, you're forgiven."

No, in forgiving our sin, Jesus Himself had to absorb the horrific punishment our sin had earned.

Hebrews 9:22 reminds us, "Without the shedding of blood there is no forgiveness." How can we begin to sound the depths of what Jesus bore on the cross in order to forgive us guilty sinners? Paul reminds us, "God made him who had no sin to be sin for us, so that in him we might become the righteousness of God" (2 Corinthians 5:21).

Jesus knew before the cross that forgiving another person's offenses is costly business. The night before He died He took the Passover cup and explained to the disciples, "This is my blood of the covenant, which is poured out for many for the forgiveness of sins" (Matthew 26:28). There is no greater expression of love. "Greater love has no one than this, that he lay down his life for his friends" (John 15:13).

Our Pardoning Love for Our Wives

A significant expression of our love for our wives is our willingness to pardon their offenses against us, whether small or marriage threatening.

Many couples choose to have 1 Corinthians 13 read as part of their wedding ceremony. Maybe you were one of them. Remember these words? "Love is patient... it is not easily angered, it keeps no record of wrongs" (1 Corinthians 13:4–5). How quickly we forget those attributes of Christlike love when our wives do things that irritate us, like locking the keys in the car—again. How do we respond when our wives do something that gets under our skin? Spout off with angry or belittling words? Erect an emotional wall, constructed of blocks of bitterness? Look for ways to pay her back by doing something we know will irritate her?

Bob Lepine reminds us of what we already know in our hearts. "The root of impatience is usually selfishness. We're not getting what we want or what we think we deserve. We don't 'suffer long'—we think we've suffered long enough!"[7] At the heart of impatience is self-serving, self-defending pride.

Patient, Pardoning Love

Loving our wives as Christ loves the church means that we express a pardoning love by being patient with our wives' offenses—small or large. If Peter's counsel in 1 Peter 4:8 is important for the body of Christ, how much more applicable is it in marriage? He writes, "Above all, love each other deeply, because love covers over a multitude of sins."

Pastor Dave Harvey reminds us how decisive patience can be: "It involves a clear-eyed realization that we may have been sinned against, and then a bold-hearted, gospel-inspired decision to cover that sin with love."[8] Why should we let our impatience continue to cloud our marriages and our reflection of Christ's love?

Forgiving, Pardoning Love

We all knew we were marrying sinners, didn't we? Before we smugly answer that, let's remember that our wives did, too. Admitting that painful reality ought to take away some of the shocked hurt when our wives sin against us. You and I are sinners who married wives who also are sinners. So, how does Christ want us to handle that?

The apostle Paul counseled the church in Colosse regarding how to handle sinful offenses within the church family: "Bear with each other and forgive whatever grievances you may have against one another" (Colossians 3:13).

Couldn't we husbands apply that same counsel in our marriages when our wives sin against us? Forgiving our wives doesn't minimize the offense. We don't sweep the matter under the rug of stoicism, pretending it doesn't hurt. David Harvey explains, "True forgiveness sees another's sin for the evil that it is, addresses it, then absorbs the cost of that sin by the power of God's abundant grace. Such forgiveness sets the sinner free; the account of the sin is closed, cancelled, blotted out."[9]

When we forgive our wives, we acknowledge that they have in some way wronged us, but even though justice may demand they pay for the suffering they've caused us, we choose not to demand payment for that debt. We let it go. We *pardon* them in love.

A young wife whom my wife and I care for deeply shared with us one day her joy of receiving her husband's forgiveness and finding restoration in their relationship. Their marriage had been sliding toward the edge of the cliff. But in God's gracious providence, because the husband made a conscious effort to reflect Christ's spirit of love and forgiveness, their slide toward dissolution stopped, and together they began their climb back up the mountain of marriage as two forgiven sinners roped together by Christ's pardoning love. She writes about it this way:

> It's hard to forgive someone who has violated your trust. After just a few short years of marriage, selfishness and pride had chipped away at the foundation of our relationship. I felt trapped and was ready to abandon my marriage and my faith to pursue what I hoped would be an opportunity for true happiness. Despite his own hurt, my husband was willing to humble himself, take ownership of his mistakes, and love and pursue me even though *I* was threatening to leave *him*. Eventually, God worked in my heart through my husband's perseverance and loving example, and today we share the rich and joyful relationship my heart had been longing for all along.

Even as our Lord has committed not to exact payment from us for our sins against Him, neither do we demand payment from our wives for their offenses against us. The offense is no longer a barrier between us as husband and wife, nor a weapon to inflict pain on our wives just because they have inflicted pain on us.

Why Should We Forgive Our Wives for Their Sins Against Us?

Let's be candid. Some husbands have been gravely wounded by their wives' sin. I have heard a husband exclaim with tear-filled eyes and tortured facial expression, "Oh, Larry. You don't know how badly she has hurt me. I am living with soul-deep wounds. How could I ever forgive her? Why should I ever forgive her? She doesn't deserve to be forgiven! If I forgive her, then I'll be condoning what she has done, and I'll never do that!"

The reason we forgive our wives is not that they *deserve* to be forgiven. So why, then?

1. *Forgive because Christ forgave you.* The message of Colossians 3:13 may be difficult to live out, but it is clear: "Forgive as the Lord forgave you." Many marriages have existed with an oppressive cloud of bitterness blocking the light of the Son because a husband stubbornly withheld forgiveness until he felt his wife earned it with sufficient remorse. But the forgiveness we extend to our wives when they sin against us is not some reward we grant them when they somehow *earn* our forgiveness.

Animosity and resentment can shackle a husband to his damaged pride, hindering him from reaching out to his wife with a pardoning love. Yet the only way to break these chains is to quit glowering at his wife's sin and gaze afresh at the undeserved pardoning love the Lord has chosen to extend to all of us. "Forgive as the Lord forgave you."

Pastor John Piper says, "Take the grace and forgiveness and justification that you have received vertically through the death of Christ and bend it out horizontally to others. Specifically, husbands to wives and wives to husbands."[10]

How many times have I offended my Lord? What if I have offended Him merely ten times each day (wishful thinking!)? That would be 70 sins each week, 3,640 crimes against the King each year, 36,400 offenses each decade of my life! Although my wife may not deserve my forgiveness, I didn't deserve the Lord's either. Yet He freely gave it, having nailed my innumerable offenses to His blood-soaked cross.

Dave Harvey gives us the bottom line: "Forgiven sinners forgive sin."[11]

2. *Forgive because you want to be forgiven on that Great Day of Judgment.* Having just taught His disciples the importance of forgiveness in what's known as The Lord's Prayer, Jesus admonished, "If you forgive men when they sin against you, your heavenly Father will also forgive you. *But if you do not forgive men their sins, your Father will not forgive your sins*" (Matthew 6:14–15, emphasis added). This sobering warning may make us uncomfortable, but we ought not dismiss its implications in order to keep our theology neat and tidy. I believe we should take the words of Jesus at face value.

How many bitter, forgiveness-withholding husbands will be shocked to hear those most-dreaded words on judgment day, "I never knew you. Away from me, you evildoers!" (Matthew 7:23)? Every husband who professes Christ should ask himself, "Would I want Jesus to treat me the same way I have treated my wife? Would I want Him to be as unforgiving to me as I have been to my wife?" I addressed this principle in *Walking Like Jesus Did:*

> Making this painful point to His Galilean listeners, Jesus told a story that has become known as "The Parable of the Unmerciful Servant" (see Matthew 18:21–35). In this story, a servant of a king was unable to pay a large debt that he owed his master. The king took pity on the man and forgave his unpayable debt. Sadly, this same servant refused to forgive a much smaller debt owed him by a fellow servant. When the king heard about his hardheartedness, he called him in a second time and rebuked him. "You wicked servant," he said, "I canceled all that debt of yours because you begged me to. Shouldn't you have had mercy on your fellow servant just as I had on you?" Jesus relates, "In anger his master turned him over to the jailers to be tortured, until he should pay back all he owed." Then the Lord adds these sobering words of application, "This is how my heavenly Father will treat each of you unless you forgive your brother from your heart" (Matthew 18:32–35).[12]

I think we could paraphrase this last verse this way: "This is how my heavenly Father will treat each of you unless you forgive your wife from your heart." Heart-challenging statement, isn't it?

How Can We Grow in a Pardoning Love?

First, we must remember whose we are and to whom we belong. Preceding Paul's command in Colossians 3:13 to forgive as the Lord forgave [us], in verse 12 he includes "identity markers," calling us "chosen," "holy," and "dearly loved." Those terms are saturated in the gospel of God's sovereign grace. In eternity past God decided to love us unconditionally and set us apart as His own trophies of grace though we did not deserve it. In turn, as we savor the joy of our own gracious pardon, we can extend a pardoning love to our wives when they offend us.

The grace of the gospel—not only for initial salvation, but for everyday life as forgiven sinners—moves us to forgive humbly, gratefully, and freely those who sin against us. To paraphrase our Lord, "He who has been forgiven much, forgives much."

Second, we must remember to whom our wives belong. The apostle Peter calls our believing wives, "heirs with you of the gracious gift of life" (1 Peter 3:7). Our Christian wives are recipients of the same pardoning love we've been given. Our Lord has poured out His mercy and grace on them, just as He has on us, no longer holding their offenses over their heads. Paul assures us, "There is now no condemnation for those who are in Christ Jesus" (Romans 8:1). Why should we husbands treat our wives any differently? Why would we refuse to forgive those whom the Lord has already forgiven?

Ruth Bell Graham, late wife of Evangelist Billy Graham, once said, "a successful marriage is the union of two forgivers."[13] With hearts saturated daily by the pardoning, life-giving gospel of Christ, let's love our wives "just as Christ loved the church and gave himself up for her" (Ephesians 5:25)—with a pardoning love.

DISCUSSION QUESTIONS AND ACTION STEPS
A Pardoning Love

Discussion Questions

1. After studying this chapter, how would you define the word "pardon"?

2. Read Romans 5:6–10. How much did you deserve Christ's forgiveness when He gave His life to forgive you? How much do you deserve His forgiveness for the sins you commit today?

3. In this chapter we talked about God's patience toward us in not "snuffing us out" for our sinful rebellion. How does this truth affect your appreciation of Christ's sacrifice for you? Read 1 Timothy 1:15–16. What was the apostle Paul's testimony regarding Christ's patience toward him?

4. Which of your wife's offenses do you find especially difficult to forgive? Why?

5. How does Christ's patience and forgiveness toward you influence how ready you are to show patience and forgiveness to your wife? Read these passages: Ephesians 4:1–2, 32, and Colossians 3:13.

6. When we demonstrate a judgmental attitude toward our wives when they sin against us, we are assuming the role of their judge. But, read Romans 12:17–19. How many seats are behind the Judge's bench? Who is sitting there? When our wives offend us and we seek vengeance instead of offering forgiveness, what are we saying about our view of God?

Action Steps

1. Think about some of your wife's weaknesses or annoying habits that "trip your trigger." Rather than discussing them with others, take them to the Lord right now and ask His forgiveness for the sinful ways you have responded in the past. Ask Him

to remind you of the magnitude of His forgiveness for your many sins, then ask Him to lead you in treating your wife with Christlike patience.

2.   Have you held grudges toward your wife's sins against you? Go to her, humbly confessing your previous hardheartedness toward her. Ask her to forgive you of your pride and stubbornness toward her. (If you are still struggling to let go of past offenses, read Matthew 6:14–15 and ask for God's help to forgive.)

13

A Persevering
Love

They were the darkest days of our marriage. It's not so much that our marriage balloon had suddenly burst into flames and crashed in some covenant-breaking unfaithfulness. It's more like it just gradually lost air over twenty years as husband and wife. In fact, the air had been escaping more rapidly of late. Now, as we look back on that most unhappy era of our married life, we can see that we had been in a downward spiral for some time. I didn't feel she was respecting me, and she didn't feel I was loving her.

One spouse's failure fueled the other's disappointment in an incessant cycle. Over time, the disappointment slid into disillusionment. My wife had already slipped into depression, and I was not far behind her, careening downward in near hopelessness. Thanks to God's grace, neither of us bailed out. How glad we are that the Lord preserved us during those darkest days, and now, also by His grace, we are entering our older years happily hand in hand.

What did the Lord use to stop our downward spiral and preserve our deflating marriage? He used simple, life-changing verses in a passage of Scripture that doesn't even deal directly with marriage. I can still recall the Holy Spirit fixing my mind and heart on these verses from 1 John 4: "This is love: not that we loved God, but that he loved us and sent his Son as an atoning sacrifice for our sins. Dear friends, since God so loved us, we also ought to love one another. ...And so we know and rely on the love God has for us. ...We love because he first loved us" (vv. 10–11, 16, 19).

The Lord began to blow the warm air of hope into my heart, turning my eyes away from what I perceived to be my wife's failures and pointing out my own prideful attempts to patch up our marriage wounds on my own. Then He riveted my eyes on His unconditional love for me through Christ's saving work on my behalf.

My love for my wife—the love that would enable me to carry through with my till-death-us-do-part vow—could not depend on how much love and respect I thought my wife was giving me, but on the certainty of God's unending love for me. It was as if the Holy Spirit was applying 1 John 4 to me very personally: "Dear Larry, since God so loved you, you also ought to love Gladine. You know and must rely not on the love and respect you perceive you are getting from her, but on the love God has for you. Since He has first loved you, Larry, now love your wife."

As the Lord renewed this hope in His persevering love for me, I committed afresh to love my wife unconditionally and unendingly. Over time God, in His mercy, began to blow the warm air of hope into my wife's heart as well, and our marriage once more began to rise and fly.

Christ's Persevering Love for His Bride

Have you ever asked, Why would Jesus continue to love the likes of me? No doubt most of us have at one time or another. We could also ask, What keeps Jesus loving His bride, the church? Is there something we can be doing—should be doing—to guarantee that He will continue to love us? What would have to happen for Jesus to decide to "divorce" us as His bride?

As we discussed in chapter 2, "A Predetermined Love," Christ does not base His love for us on any conditions in *us*. It's entirely within Himself. He decided ahead of time to love us, knowing we would disappoint Him time and time again. "You see," Paul writes, "at just the right time, when we were still powerless, Christ died for the ungodly. Very rarely will anyone die for a righteous man, though for a good man someone might possibly dare to die. But God demonstrates his own love for us in this: While we were still sinners, Christ died for us" (Romans 5:6–8).

No person, power, or circumstance could ever change the Lord's commitment to love His bride. Listen to the passionate assurance from the pen of Paul: "I am convinced that neither death nor life, neither angels nor demons, neither the present nor the future, nor any powers, neither height nor depth, nor anything else in all creation, will be able to separate us from the love of God that is in Christ Jesus our Lord" (Romans 8:38–39).

Christ's love for us is not only unconditional but unending. Nothing will ever come up that could cause Jesus to go back on His pledge to love us. Psalm 136 repeats the words *His love endures forever*" in all 26 verses. Christ will never abandon us. The 17th Century author Thomas Watson uses the word picture that the church will also never be widowed.[1] Christ's love for His bride is a permanent, *persevering* love.

Our Persevering Love for Our Wives

Are we committed to loving our wives as Christ loves the church with a persevering love—come what may? I doubt that many of us were intentionally lying on our wedding day when we pledged to love our brides "until death us do part" or "so long as we both shall live." I assume we meant those words, even if we hadn't given much thought beforehand about what trials and temptations could lie ahead.

So what keeps us from persevering? Why do so many marriages end in divorce? It's tempting to defend ourselves with victim language, as if things over which we had no control just happened to us. We've all heard the laments: "I guess we just have irreconcilable differences," or "We just fell out of love," or "The stress of staying married to her just got to be too much."

Pastor Alistair Begg comments on this crucial wedding pledge, "So long as you both shall live": "Despite the clarity of this concluding statement of the wedding vow, an alarming number of couples apparently determine that this part is optional. Instead of facing difficulties and setbacks with a 'for life' mentality, they are immediately on the lookout for loopholes and escape clauses."[2]

Haven't you seen that also? Too many couples no longer view marriage as permanent. They figuratively or literally replace the vow "so long as you both shall live" with "as long as we both shall love," or "as long as we both are happy." When the passions die or the stresses increase or someone more appealing comes along, one spouse or the other picks up the phone to make that first appointment with the divorce attorney.

In one of Satan's great deceptions, the costs of pursuing a divorce appear less than the costs of staying in the marriage. The Christian community's increasing acceptance of divorce as a viable option for hurting marriages smooths the path to the divorce courts. In the name of Christian compassion many pastors, counselors and writers allow divorce as a legitimate way to end the pain of a marriage gone bad.

This widespread acceptance of divorce is nothing new. Jesus confronted the religious leaders of His day about their lax view on divorce. The Pharisees tried to put Jesus in a no-win situation by asking Him what they perceived to be a very difficult question: "Is it lawful for a man to divorce his wife for any and every reason?" (Matthew 19:3).

Here's some background regarding the tricky question of acceptable grounds for divorce—then and now. *Some* Jews followed the relatively conservative thinking of Rabbi Shammai, who taught that unchastity or adultery provided the only proper ground for divorce. Others, however, followed the more lenient views of Rabbi Hillel, who taught that there were many legitimate reasons for a man to divorce his wife.

Would Jesus weigh in on this controversy? The Pharisee interrogators apparently assumed they had Jesus cornered. If He took the conservative position, He would lose favor with the liberals. If he sided with the liberals, the conservatives would ostracize him. So how did Jesus respond?

He never took the bait. He went straight to the Scriptures to remind His hearers of God's teaching regarding the foundational unity and permanence of marriage. Jesus asked them, "Haven't you read...?" no doubt to expose their sinful motives and lack of submission to God's Word. What mattered to Jesus—and what should matter to us—is the clear teaching of Scripture, no matter how uncomfortable it makes us, no matter how it differs from opinions of any popular Christian psychologist or preacher.

Jesus basically told the Pharisees, "You're asking the wrong question. You should be asking, 'How can I live in submission to God's teaching of the permanence of marriage?'" The Pharisees focused on excuses for divorce while Jesus focused on reasons to *persevere* in our marriage commitment.

See God's Design from the Beginning

The Lord reminded His hearers of Scripture's first passages about God's design for marriage, marriage as it was "supposed to be." Referring back to Genesis 1 and 2, Jesus says essentially, "Look at this 'before' picture." Understanding the before-the-fall model—before sin messed things up—will help us understand God's ideal.

Jesus referred to Genesis 2:24, which says, "A man will leave his father and mother and be united to his wife, and they will become one flesh." The Hebrew verb for "be united" implies being strongly attached. Think of it as "The husband shall be superglued to his wife."

That concept then leads us to Jesus' reiteration, "The two will become one flesh" (Matthew 19:3). This phrase implies unity, not only physically but relationally. These two people—a husband and a wife—have, in effect, become "one person."

By the way, that's why people who are going through divorce often describe feeling as if they are being torn apart. They are. Divorce rips apart this "one flesh" that God intended to be permanent.

Having drawn His hearers' attention to this pre-sin-infected-world's ideal marriage, Jesus then concludes, "So they are no longer two but one" (v. 6). Jesus was strongly impressing upon the people God's original design regarding the permanence of marriage. Then, if we may paraphrase our Lord, Jesus commands, "Since it is God who has made this permanent union, since it is God who has made these two people one, stop your practice of divorcing your wives!"

Stop Looking for Loopholes

I strongly believe that we need to hear this command from King Jesus in our evangelical churches today. We have wrongly spent too much time and energy trying to find loopholes for divorce and have lost sight of God's design for permanence. Marriage is for keeps.

Jesus briefly explained in Matthew 19:8–9 that biblical laws regarding divorce don't exist because God is somehow pro divorce. He led Moses to write laws governing divorce and remarriage only because He knew people's hearts can become callous toward the sanctity and permanence of marriage that He instituted. God designed marriage to be "until death us do part." Jesus believed and taught that truth despite opposition and despite its unpopularity. Do we?

Some time ago a friend of my wife's, a sister in Christ, was struggling in her marriage. Her unconverted husband was largely uninvolved in her life. As is all too common, he would go to work, come home, plop down on the couch, and watch TV while he ate his supper alone. Hours later he would crawl into bed and quickly fall asleep, only to follow the same solitary routine again the next day.

Understandably, she grew soul weary of this isolation from the man with whom she was supposed to have a relationship. People close to her encouraged her to divorce her husband. But the Holy Spirit didn't give her any peace about following through with this counsel.

One day she stopped by our home to ask Gladine's advice. She recounted for my wife her frustration and indecision. "I just wish God would write in the sky the answer to what I'm supposed to do," she said.

Gladine opened her Bible to 1 Corinthians 7:10, slid it across the dining room table so it faced her friend, and asked her to read the verse aloud.

"A wife must not separate from her husband," her friend read. Then she let out a shriek and said, "There it is! In black and white! There's my answer in God's Word!"

God saved that marriage. In fact, in His amazing grace, He saved that husband, and today they are happily united in Christ.

Clear. Straightforward: "A wife must not separate from her husband." Then Paul continues in that passage, "And a husband must not divorce his wife" (v. 11). Oh, that we would spend less time and energy looking for ways *out* of our marriages and spend more time and energy (and prayer!) seeking to *keep* our wedding vows "until death us do part!"

Don't Believe the Relief Fallacy

Not only is divorce displeasing to God, but it almost never delivers its promised relief from the pain of a difficult marriage. In the fictional world of entertainment, adultery and divorce are often portrayed as something desirable, some form of fun liberation from a boring or annoying marriage. Yet are people who have divorced, in fact, better off? Well-known author and speaker Charles Colson observes, "A study that examined the impact of divorce ten years after the divorce found that among two-thirds of divorced couples, one partner is still depressed and financially precarious. And among a quarter of all divorced couples, *both* former partners are worse off, suffering loneliness and depression."[3]

Not only are the husband and wife negatively impacted by divorce, but the pain and disruption spill into the lives of the children, extended families on both sides, close friends, the local church, and even the reputation of Christ.

Would you really be better off in the long run by bailing out rather than working on a hurting marriage and persevering to keep your marriage vows? Lou Priolo wisely counsels, "Unless you truly have biblical grounds for divorce, it's much easier to endure whatever it takes to repair this marriage than to run away from it and start all over again. If it's a fresh start you want, why not start being the kind of husband the Bible requires of you?"[4]

When, in those darkest days, we feel that quitting would be better than having to endure for one more day the suffering of a painful marriage, we need to remember that we are not alone. We are not the first husbands to experience this pain. Radio preacher Chuck Swindoll admits, "Of course it's difficult! For sure, there will be times you are inwardly convinced you can't go on. But I remind you of your vow, your stated commitment: 'For better, for worse.' What you are experiencing may be some of the 'worse.' And no marriage is exempt from such times."[5]

Seek God's Help to Persevere

Why do we assume that the Christian life is to be free of suffering? That goal may drive our narcissistic culture, and it might be what our flesh craves, but God has not called us to a suffering-free life this side of Glory. In fact, 1 Peter 2:21 says that we have been *called* to suffer, "because Christ suffered for you, leaving you an example, that you should follow in his steps." Rather than searching for avenues *out* of suffering (divorce?), we need to commit ourselves to taking our painful situations and entrusting them to our heavenly Father. He will strengthen us. He sees our pain. He understands what we are going through.[6]

Gladine and I have found, as have other couples, that when both husband and wife remain committed to the marriage vows, eventually we will begin to come out the other side of this deep valley of suffering. Once again, by God's grace, the rays of the Lord's sunshine will begin to warm your marriage and rekindle the feelings of love. This is God's gracious gift borne out of a commitment to keep the marriage covenant through those darkest days.

So let's commit to reflecting our covenant-keeping Lord's relationship to His Bride, persevering in our marriage vows, "for better or for worse, for richer, for poorer, in sickness and in health, to love and to cherish; from this day forward until death do us part."

Banish the D word from your vocabulary—even when you're in a heated argument with your wife. Commit to working tirelessly through your difficulties.

I was fascinated to read about the longest-married couple (at that time), Percy and Florence Arrowsmith of England. In 2005 they celebrated their 80th wedding anniversary! In an interview about this unparalleled milestone, Mrs. Arrowsmith commented, "It has not been easy but worth every minute because he is much more than my best friend: he is the love of my life. ...It is all about hard work. We have had our arguments, but we work through them together. We always go to bed as friends and always make up before we go to sleep with a kiss and a cuddle."[7] Amazing! After 80 years, this couple was still committed to working on their marriage. That's persevering love!

"What God has joined together, let man not separate" (Mark 10:9).

DISCUSSION QUESTIONS AND ACTION STEPS
A Persevering Love

Discussion Questions

1. Read Matthew 19:1–12. Discuss the similarities of the divorce debate in Jesus' day to the discussions we have in evangelical churches today on this issue.

2. It's been noted that the divorce rate within the evangelical church is not different from American society at large. Why do you think that is? What can be done, by God's grace, to begin reversing the high divorce rate within the church?

3. Have you ever felt like calling it quits in your own marriage? What was happening at that time in your life? What has the Lord used to keep you committed to your marriage?

4. If you are currently in a second (or subsequent) marriage, in what ways do you want this marriage to be different?

Action Steps

1. Ask your wife if there are times when she does not feel secure in your commitment to her. If she says there are such times, humbly and without defensiveness ask her what changes she would like to see you make to reassure her of your commitment.

2. Have you ever threatened your wife with divorce, even in the heat of an argument? If so, confess to her that you were wrong to make such a threat. Ask her to forgive you for saying that. Assure her that you fully intend to keep your marriage vows till death.

3. Read 1 John 4:7–21 together with your wife. Thank the Lord for His unfailing love for you. Ask Him to refresh your souls with reminders of His love as you seek to love each other by relying on the love He has for you.

4. At your next anniversary, plan a recommitment ceremony, renewing your vows to each other.

14

The Challenges and Rewards of Christlike Love

It's quite the high calling—to love our wives just as Christ loved the church and gave Himself up for her—isn't it? Yet Jesus Christ, the Perfect Husband, has called us to reflect *His* love for *His* bride by loving *our* brides in similar ways:

Just as He loved His bride with a predetermined, peerless, practical love, so must we.

Just as He loved His bride with a protecting, purposeful, providing love, so must we.

Just as He loved His bride with a passionate, praying, purifying love, so must we.

Just as He loved His bride with a pardoning, persevering love, so must we.

Challenges

Any of you feeling as I am about now—a bit inadequate? How about extremely inadequate? How are we ever going to fulfill this God-given commission to love our wives as Christ loves the church? Oh, we feel good about some encouraging aspects of our marriages, but there are plenty of husbanding deficiencies we would just as soon not be reminded about—especially by our wives.

The Challenge of Inadequacy

Author, counselor, and speaker Jay Adams speaks for all of us who feel inadequate:

It is plainly too much. The task is too great for sinful, weak human beings. You know that you cannot fulfill this commandment. It is only as the Spirit of God works in your life that you can begin to approximate the Lord's loving leadership over His church. Yet you must aspire to nothing less in your relationship to your wife. ...You must emulate Him in all your ways. To be like Jesus Christ in relationship to your wife is an enormous order to fill.[1]

What's it going to take for us to overcome our failures, to grow out of our deficiencies, and become husbands who love our wives with a Christlike love? Do we just suck it up and try harder? Will learning a few new communication skills or lovemaking techniques do the trick? Maybe the key for us to be better husbands is getting our spouses to become better wives. If they were just more appreciative or responsive to our husbandly efforts, of course, we would be better husbands, right?

Actually, men, there is only one answer. It's simple yet profound: God's love for us. Could we paraphrase the apostle John when he writes, "We love [our wives] because he first loved us" (1 John 4:19)? Christian educator Bryan Chapell reminds us, "The ultimate resource we have...is Christ's love for us. ...When we rest in his love, we can reflect it. The degree of confidence we have in the strength of his care for us will largely determine the measure of selfless tenderness we can express."[2]

The Challenge of Insufficient Resources

If we liken our love to life-giving water, our calling is to give that water to our thirsty wives. But where would we get our own water tanks filled so we have enough to share? Let's be candid. For many of us, our own spiritual and emotional tanks are running on empty. What do we tend to do when we are told to love our wives while our own tanks are nearly dry? We may try to pressure our wives to pour love into our tanks so we can dispense love back to them. But if they don't or can't meet our demands, we may defend our failure, blaming *their* failure to adequately love us. The sad result is that both husband and wife run low on love, each failing to pour love into the other's life in sufficient quantities to have enough love to give back.

The bottom line, brothers, is that we cannot and should not depend on our wives to be the primary fillers of our love tanks. Instead, we need to ask our more-than-gracious Lord to fill us. Gary Ricucci, coauthor of *Love that Lasts*, sums it up this way: "We can love and lead our wives because, and only because, Christ first loved us (Galatians 2:20). Our role originates *in* the gospel, is empowered *by* the gospel, and is perfected *through* the gospel. We can love and lead our wives because our Savior, Jesus Christ, loved us, gave himself up for us, and leads us each day in mercy and grace."[3]

- Christ's love for us is as adequate as His sacrifice on the cross.
- Christ's love for us is as constant and consistent as His gospel.
- Christ's love for us is as sure on our worst days as it is on our best days.

We must saturate our minds and hearts with the overwhelming truth of the gospel—the gospel that we need, not only in coming to Christ for initial salvation, but the gospel we need in living out our salvation every day. "Nothing is more essential to a marriage, and nothing brings more hope, than applying the gospel of Jesus Christ."[4]

The Resources Available to Us

So how do we apply the gospel to our marriages? How do we keep growing in loving our wives as Christ loves the church?

1. By continually reminding ourselves of the reality of the love God has already shown us in Jesus Christ. The apostle John makes it very clear. "This is love: not that we loved God, but that he loved us and sent his Son as an atoning sacrifice for our sins. Dear friends, since God so loved us, we also ought to love one another. ... And so we know and rely on the love God has for us" (1 John 4:10–11, 16). We love our wives by drawing from the never-ending love that the Lord has shown us.

2. By staying involved and accountable within the local church. We need to admit humbly that we cannot go it alone. We need brothers and sisters in Christ who will remind us with their words and lives that we, too, must depend on the gospel for life and marriage.

Make or renew your commitment to being involved in a Bible-believing, Christ-exalting, gospel-saturated local church. Look for peers who will walk this journey of married life with you. Find a mentor who will model a Christ-reflecting marriage.

Husband-wife authors Gary and Betsy Ricucci make this helpful comparison: "Sanctification—becoming like Christ—is indeed a community project. And marriage, growing to represent Christ and the church, is every bit as much a community project."[5]

We need the local church.

Rewards

Why commit to this life-long quest of loving our wives as Christ loves the church? What are the benefits?

1. Our wives benefit. As we reflect Christ's love to our wives, we are serving them, helping them to become more like our precious Savior. Church leader C. J. Mahaney predicts that, "as you learn more and more how to love and lead your wife as Christ does the church…your wife will become more full of joy, hope and peace and will radiate more of the love and grace of God in all she does."[6]

Someday, in the December of our lives, we want, by God's grace, to be able to look into the faces of those women we have long loved and hear them say to us, "Thank you, dear. I am more like Christ today, having been married to you all these years."

2. We husbands benefit. As we love our wives with Christlike love, our wives become more spiritually beautiful. And that is a boon to us as well. When we become more lovingly involved in our wives' lives, they become more like Jesus, and they, in turn, enrich our lives.

In a sense, we're doing ourselves a favor when we love our wives as Christ loves His church. Is not this the implication of Ephesians 5:28: "In this same way, husbands ought to love their wives as their own bodies. He who loves his wife loves himself"?

3. The reputation of Christ in this fallen world benefits. Our marriages are a living reflection—a daily re-enactment—of the love Christ demonstrates to His bride, the church. Much of what our biblically illiterate society knows of Christ it learns from watching how we, as followers of Christ, live our everyday lives—especially in the context of our marriages and families.

Consider these motivating words from Bryan Chapell:

Living as a Christian family in the midst of a godless society has transforming power. Church historians say that
Christianity swept the ancient Roman world not so much
because of the arguments of theologians but because of the
infectious love evident in Christian families. This spiritual
contagion can spread again. As Christ's love changes our
families, it also appeals to outsiders who are desperate for
answers to their own family problems.[7]

Let's fix our eyes on our Savior and love our wives as Christ loves
His church. Let's look forward to hearing on that Great Day the
most blessed words any husband could hear: "Well done, good and
faithful husband! You reflected My love for My bride! Come and
share your Master's happiness!"[8]

DISCUSSION QUESTIONS AND ACTION STEPS
Christlike Love's Challenges & Rewards

Discussion Questions

1. Read Ephesians 5:25–33 again. What about Christ's love for His bride especially grips you?

2. In what key ways has God been at work in your life through this study of *Loving Your Wife as Christ Loves the Church*?

3. What encouraging changes have you seen in your marriage since you began this study?

4. What is your plan for giving priority to your ministry of loving your wife as Christ loves the church?

Action Steps

1. If you are not already part of a Bible-teaching, Christ-centered, gospel-saturated church, talk with your wife about finding one that you can call home. Ask the Lord to lead you to a church that will be an encouragement to your marriage.

2. Lay out a plan with your accountability partner(s) for continuing to meet on a regular basis for encouraging one another in your ministry of husbanding. When and where will you meet? What will be the focus of your time together? (See Appendix D for ideas on forming a men's accountability group.)

3. As a group, spend some time thanking the Lord for His gracious involvement as you have worked through ways to love your wives as Christ loves the church. Ask for His continued grace in molding you to reflect His love, growing in your relationship with your wife and your ministry to her.

Appendix A

A Personal Relationship with God

Maybe you've been reading this book about loving your wife in a Christlike way, yet you've never personally experienced the love of Christ. It's impossible to reflect Christ's love to your wife if you have not first let Christ's love shine into your own soul in a life-transforming, eternity-changing way. And having a right relationship with God is even more important than having a good relationship with your wife. God wants a personal relationship with you, so He makes these important truths clear in His Word:

The reason we exist has more to do with God than it does us.
Each of us was born with a "job description." The Bible clearly teaches that God designed you and me to reflect His glory with all that we are, with all we have, and with all that we do in life (Isaiah 43:7). He created us to find our greatest joy in seeking His smile and His honor in all things.

Not one of us can, on our own, do what God designed us for.
Even though God designed us to seek His glory in all things, we have sought our own honor instead. Even though God created us to find our greatest joy in Him, we have ignored Him and sought satisfaction in our own possessions, power, and pleasure.

Isaiah 53:6 gives this painful diagnosis of our condition before God: "We all, like sheep, have gone astray, each of us has turned to his own way." Jesus Christ has been the single exception to this failure, and there has never been another, since sin entered the human race at the time of our great, great-grandparents (many times over), Adam and Eve. "For all have sinned and fall short of the glory of God" (Romans 3:23).

God has every right to condemn us because of our willful rebellion.

Our rebellion against God—seeking our own glory instead of His, seeking satisfaction in our own possessions instead of in Him, and desiring power and pleasure instead of Him—is inexcusable. It separates us from our Creator. We're not separated from God because we don't know anything about Him. The Bible says, "What may be known about God is plain to them, because God has made it plain to them. For since the creation of the world God's invisible qualities—his eternal power and divine nature—have been clearly seen, being understood from what has been made, so that men are without excuse" (Romans 1:19–20).

Instead, we're separated from God because we don't want Him in our lives. Our refusal to honor God and find our joy in Him is open rebellion against the God who made us. The Bible calls that rebellion sin, and sin rightfully earns God's condemnation: "The wages of sin is death" (Romans 6:23). And the ultimate death is to be eternally separated from God in a place of real, conscious torment known as hell or the lake of fire. Paul teaches that those who do not know God "will be punished with everlasting destruction and shut out from the presence of the Lord" (2 Thessalonians 1:9).

We do not have the ability to fix our terrible dilemma.

God's standard of acceptance is perfection—sinlessness. The Bible teaches that God "cannot tolerate wrong" (Habakkuk 1:13). Yet, we've all sinned (Romans 3:23). No amount of good works and no amount of religious devotion can compensate for or eradicate our sin and its guilt before the perfectly sinless God who made us and holds us accountable. In fact, even our attempts to justify ourselves before God are offensive to Him. He looks at them as "filthy rags" (Isaiah 64:6). We can't *work* our way out of our guilt and into God's good graces, so our situation seems hopeless.

God, Himself, has provided the only solution to our terrible dilemma.

The bad news is that we're undeniably, helplessly guilty before God. But the good news is that what *we* wouldn't and couldn't do, *God* did.

Paul tells us that "what the law was powerless to do in that it was weakened by the sinful nature, God did by sending his own Son in the likeness of sinful man to be a sin offering. And so he condemned sin in sinful man, in order that the righteous requirements of the law might be fully met in us" (Romans 8:3-4).

Jesus Christ, God's unique Son, came to this earth to keep all of God's laws perfectly. He did for us what we should have done but couldn't do by ourselves. He perfectly and consistently glorified God the Father. Then Jesus also solved our terrible dilemma of guilt by taking on Himself the "wages of sin" we deserved. He did this by dying on a cross as a substitute for guilty sinners, such as you and me. "God made him [Jesus Christ] who had no sin to be sin for us, so that in him we might become the righteousness of God" (2 Corinthians 5:21).

As living proof that Jesus' sacrifice on the cross for us satisfied our holy God's requirements, God raised Jesus from the dead. Paul says Jesus "was raised to life for our justification" (Romans 4:25).

Christ's work on the cross opened the door for us to have a right relationship with God.

God graciously calls us to repent of (turn from) our sin and all our attempts to justify ourselves in His eyes. If we ever want to be right with God, we must put all our hope in Jesus Christ alone. The Bible says, "Salvation is found in no one else, for there is no other name under heaven given to men by which we must be saved" (Acts 4:12). And "If you confess with your mouth, 'Jesus is Lord,' and believe in your heart that God raised him from the dead, you will be saved. For it is with your heart that you believe and are justified, and it is with your mouth that you confess and are saved. As the Scripture says, 'Anyone who trusts in him will never be put to shame'" (Romans 10:9–11).

How will you respond?

Is God doing something in your heart right now? Do you sense your sinfulness before the holy God who made you? Do you want to be right with Him? Why don't you talk to God right now and ask Him to forgive your sin and to make you His son? Trust in Jesus Christ and what He accomplished on the cross, and He will do it.

He is gracious beyond your wildest imagination. "To all who received him [Jesus Christ], to those who believed in his name, he gave the right to become children of God—children born not of natural descent, nor of human decision or a husband's will, but born of God" (John 1:12–13).

God wants you to grow in your relationship with Him.

If you have put your trust in Christ for a right relationship with God, let me encourage you to do several things:

1. Begin reading God's Word on a regular basis. That's how you get to know Him better and understand what it means to live for His glory. Not sure where to start? You might want to begin with the Gospel of Mark (the second book in the New Testament section of the Bible).

2. Get into the habit of talking to God each day. He wants you to grow in your relationship with Him and talking to Him (and listening to Him) is very important.

3. Find a church in your community that has an obvious commitment to knowing Christ through the faithful teaching of the Bible—if you're not in one already. Tell some of the leaders what God has been doing in your life and ask them for their help in your spiritual growth.

This is my prayer for you: *"May the God of peace, who through the blood of the eternal covenant brought back from the dead our Lord Jesus, that great Shepherd of the sheep, equip you with everything good for doing his will, and may he work in us what is pleasing to him, through Jesus Christ, to whom be glory for ever and ever. Amen"* (Hebrews 13:20–21).

Appendix B

For the Man With an Unconverted Wife

There are plenty of stories about the Christian woman who has an unconverted husband, one who hasn't put his trust in Christ as Savior. But what about marriages in which it's the other way around? Too often we neglect the topic of how a believing man is to live with his unbelieving wife. We can be thankful that the Bible addresses this situation in 1 Corinthians 7:12. The apostle Paul begins, "If any brother has a wife who is not a believer... ."

If you are a follower of Jesus Christ but your wife isn't, you are not alone. There are couples who both were unconverted at the time of their weddings, and later the husband was saved but not the wife. A number of men have married someone who claimed to know Christ, only to find out later that her profession of faith was merely insincere words uttered to get the man to marry her. Some Christian men—maybe hoping that the spiritual situation would improve after the wedding—knowingly chose to marry their sweethearts who were still without Christ.

Biblical principles guide us in all three situations.

First, it's important to note that the Christian man who knowingly married a non-Christian needs to deal with his disobedience to the clear command of 2 Corinthians 6:14: "Do not be yoked together with unbelievers. For what do righteousness and wickedness have in common? Or what fellowship can light have with darkness?" If this is your case, have you confessed your disobedience to the Lord? If so, please be assured of His forgiveness (1 John 1:9). If He has forgiven you, you are indeed forgiven. You are not living in some state of perpetual sin that needs to be forgiven over and over.

Second, regardless of how you came to be married to a woman who is not a believer, you need to realize that your situation does have its peculiar difficulties. As 2 Corinthians 6:15 pointedly asks, "What does a believer have in common with an unbeliever?"

- *A Christian and a non-Christian have very different value systems by which they live and make decisions.* The Christian lives with a "vertical orientation." He treasures Christ above all else and seeks His glory in all of life and eternity. The non-Christian lives with a "horizontal orientation," living for this current life and seeking happiness and purpose through the things this world offers.

- *A believer and a nonbeliever have different priorities in life.* For example, the believing husband loves the people of Christ and naturally wants to be involved in the life of the church family. The non-Christian wife may have no such desire. The Christian husband may greatly enjoy giving financially to the expansion of Christ's kingdom, a priority his unbelieving wife finds unnecessary at best and foolish at worst. Certain forms of entertainment he and his wife may have enjoyed in the days before he knew Christ may repulse the converted husband, while his unconverted wife feels no similar revulsion. Most significantly for many "mixed" marriages, the Christian husband and non-Christian wife may have very different concepts regarding how to rear their children. He wants to "bring them up in the training and instruction of the Lord" (Ephesians 6:4), but she feels no such desire.

So how is a Christian man supposed to live peaceably with a non-Christian wife? Commit yourself to loving her in the following ways:

- *Pray persistently.* Sometimes a Christian husband tries to coerce his wife's conversion through forceful logic or emotional pressure. While we obviously desire the conversion of these dear unbelieving women we love, we will not win them merely by our logic or emotional appeals. Unsaved people—including your wife—are neither able (1 Corinthians 2:14) nor willing (Romans 8:7) to understand spiritual truths and seek God. God must do His miracle of saving grace in their lives if they are to join us as believers.

With this in mind, devote yourself to praying for your wife's conversion and for your own ministry of declaring and displaying saving grace to her. As a backwoods Christian man once exclaimed in this simple but profound way, "If God don't turn on the lights, they don't get turned on!" Persistently ask the Lord to "turn on the lights" for your wife.

- *Live consistently.* We're all hypocrites in some ways, but as much as you can, by God's grace, consistently reflect the character of Christ in your daily life. Your marriage is a legitimate marriage in the eyes of God. He cares about your relationship with her. Seek to honor the Lord in your home by providing a godly influence. 1 Corinthians 7:14 addresses this influence we have when it says, "The unbelieving wife has been sanctified through her believing husband."

- *Love unconditionally.* Loving a person with radically different priorities and passions has its challenges, but seek to love your wife without conditions. Assure her of your unswerving commitment and devotion to her even though she doesn't share your commitment to the Savior. Paul writes, "If any brother has a wife who is not a believer and she is willing to live with him, he must not divorce her" (1 Corinthians 7:12). Never threaten your wife with divorce. She should live in the assurance and safety of your lifelong commitment to her. Tell her frequently of your undying love. *Show* her your unswerving loyalty *daily*.

- *Lead gently.* Being a Christian husband means leading your home in the ways of Christ, even if your wife doesn't wholeheartedly support you in it. You still have the responsibility to provide spiritual leadership to your wife and children. Without

becoming mean-spirited or belligerent, initiate family devotions and involvement in a Christ-honoring local church. If
your wife will consent to being involved, wonderful! However,
even if she chooses not to participate, gently lead your children
in the ways of Christ.

If your wife is open to it, share what you're learning in your own Bible
reading, what the Lord has taught you from your pastor's sermons, or
what answers to prayer you've received. But don't preach or force on
your wife spiritual lessons she is not open to hear.

Following the biblical principles we've looked at in this book,
we might apply Peter's counsel for converted wives with unconverted
husbands (1 Peter 3:1–2) to the opposite situation, paraphrasing it
like this: "Husbands, in the same way love your wives as Christ loves
the church so that, if any of them do not believe the word, they may
be won over without words by the behavior of their husbands, when
they see the sacrificial love and humble service of your lives."

But, what if your unconverted wife insists on leaving you? What
is God's call on your life in that painful situation? The Word of God
gives this counsel: "If the unbeliever leaves, let him do so. A believing
man or woman is not bound in such circumstances; God has called
us to live in peace. How do you know, wife, whether you will save
your husband? Or, how do you know, husband, whether you will
save your wife?" (1 Corinthians 7:15–16).

In other words, even if you don't want your unsaved wife to
leave, God's Word calls you to respond with peace. Don't make it
ugly. With sadness of heart and calm trust in the Lord, let her go.
In your pain, remember this promise from God: "'Never will I leave
you; never will I forsake you.' So we say with confidence, 'The Lord is
my helper; I will not be afraid. What can man do to me?'" (Hebrews
13:5–6).

Appendix C

For the Man in a
Particularly Difficult Marriage

Let's face it. Every marriage is difficult. Personally, I think those who describe their marriages as low maintenance may either be lying or living in shallow relationships, never facing the deeper issues of the heart.

Every marriage has its difficulties. What else would we expect from a union of two sinners? A sinful man married to a sinful woman share a home, bank accounts, and a bed, day in and day out, year after year. But some marriages are *particularly* difficult.

Perhaps you are in a marriage on life support. You've been staring at the marriage monitors, wondering when your relationship is going to flat line.

How did you get here? What happened to that love you and your wife once felt so passionately for each other?

- Has your marriage been suffering a slow death? Is your home permeated with the cold silence of a morgue? Do the two of you feel like emotional corpses?

- At the other extreme, is your marriage loud and volatile? Have way too many red-hot accusations and arguments driven you farther and farther away from the oneness of life the two of you once embraced?

- Has adultery—yours, hers, or both—sucked the life-breath out of your marriage?

No matter how you arrived in the pit of matrimonial despair, my hunch is that you still have at least a flicker of desire to revive your marriage. Otherwise you wouldn't be reading this. So what can a husband do when his marriage seems particularly difficult?

Here are some biblical steps to help you move forward in this quest:

1. Rekindle Hope.

Husband-wife coauthors Bill and Pam Farrel remind us, "It's not hopeless! Rebuilding relationships is not easy, but it can be done."[1] You won't find hope by trying to muster up inside yourself some Little-Orphan-Annie-like wishful "the sun will come up tomorrow" stuff. You won't find hope by determining to get your wife to change. The breath of new life for your marriage doesn't depend on your wife but on the Lord Himself.

True hope comes only from the Lord and His persistent grace. Marriage conference speakers Dennis and Barbara Rainey remind us, "God is the One who changes hearts, revives marriages, heals wounds, and breathes life into lifeless relationships."[2]

Remember what you were like spiritually when the Lord saved you? You were not just a little bit sick spiritually. You were dead! God's Word teaches, "As for you, you were dead in your transgressions and sins" (Ephesians 2:1). Humanly speaking, you were a hopeless case. You were spiritually dead, unable and unwilling to do anything to resolve your own spiritual dilemma of being estranged from God. But what did God do? "Because of his great love for us, God, who is rich in mercy, *made us alive* with Christ even when we were dead in transgressions—it is by grace you have been saved" (Ephesians 2:4–5, emphasis added).

Isn't this same gracious Lord who miraculously gave life to your dead soul also able to give life miraculously to your dead marriage? If He can save a sinner like you, can't He save a marriage like yours? Thank Him for the saving grace He has already shown you. Thank Him for the sustaining grace He gives you every day to live in this particularly difficult marriage. Ask Him to give you grace to be the kind of husband who reflects His love for His bride as you seek to love your wife, even when loving her seems so unappreciated or unrequited.

Ask Him. Ask humbly. Ask desperately. Ask persistently. As you learn more and more to look to Him and lean on Him in this particularly difficult marriage, watch how He gently begins to rekindle hope in your heart.

2. Recall Your New-Love Days.

Cooling love is nothing new. We even see it in the Book of Revelation. In Jesus' message to the church, His bride, at Ephesus, he says, "I hold this against you: You have forsaken your first love. Remember the height from which you have fallen!" (Revelation 2:4–5).

Can you remember better days in your marriage? A season when your relationship with your wife was that of two lovebirds passionate about each other? Recalling the good times in your past can help you face the future with revived hope. If such recollections create a growing longing in your heart to restore that lost love, that's good. Don't squelch that longing. Don't cynically dismiss it, reasoning that you can't recapture what you once had. Keep your hope in the Lord to restore your lost love.

3. Express Your Remorse.

Unfortunately, the word *remorse* has fallen out of common use in our conscience-seared culture. Remorse carries the idea of a deep sense of guilt or regret for our actions or attitudes. I think the key here is that we are conscious of our own sins against the Lord and against our wives and that we deeply regret what we have done.

Several years ago, while meeting with a friend in the early stages of restoring a marriage rocked by his wife's adultery, I was encouraged to hear him speak brokenly about his own failures—the sin of ignoring his wife and not pursuing her in love. My hope grew for this couple as I realized that not only was he expressing his own pain of being sinned against by his wife but also his deep regret for his own part in their marriage's difficulties. He was truly remorseful, and that pleases God.

God is committed to coming to the aid of people who are truly remorseful over their own sins, to those who do not justify themselves by focusing on how others have sinned against them. Consider these encouraging words from Isaiah 57:15: "I live in a high and holy place, but also with him who is contrite and lowly in spirit, to revive the spirit of the lowly and to revive the heart of the contrite."

That's good news for hurting husbands, isn't it? Have you reflected on your own contribution to your marriage troubles? Have you "owned" your sin? Has your heart been broken with remorse over your sin against God and against your wife? If not, why not stop right now and ask the Lord to break your heart and show you your sin?

4. Repent of Your Sin.

Repentance is related to *remorse* yet different. Remorse pertains to our feelings, whereas repentance deals also with our actions. Repentance is a radical shift in outlook that leads to a radical shift in behavior. As a man is gripped by true remorse over his own damaging contribution to his hurting marriage, his life will take a radical turn. His former sinful pride begins to melt under a new God-pleasing humility. And this new humility begins to show in some important ways within the marriage relationship.

Pride moves a man to seek to justify himself in his wife's eyes and even God's. Self-justification can consume him. Pride never welcomes the powerful, transforming grace of God. In fact, it invites God's resistance. Peter teaches that "God opposes the proud but gives grace to the humble" (1 Peter 5:5).

By God's grace, the repentant husband *stops playing defense* against his wife. Aware of his own sinfulness, he entrusts himself into the hands of our gracious Lord.

The repentant husband also *stops playing offense* against his wife. I can still recall a painfully frustrating interaction with my wife. Exasperated with not getting things my way, I finally exclaimed, "I can't win!" After an awkward few seconds of silence she asked, "Is that what you want? To win?"

The Lord used my wife's probing question to get my attention. What was my goal? Why was I playing offense against her? What was I hoping to accomplish by persistently pointing out her supposed sins against me? Her sanctification and God's glory? Or convincing her "I'm the good guy and you're the bad guy here." Self-protecting, self-promoting pride does so much damage and invites God's resistance. If we want to see our particularly difficult marriages restored, we must repent of our sinful pride and let humility do its work of softening our hearts, our words, and our actions.

5. Re-court Your Wife.

Jesus called the church at Ephesus not only to repent but also to "do the things you did at first" (Revelation 2:5). This is good advice for husbands in difficult marriages. Do you remember how you once courted your wife? How you thoughtfully did things and said things to woo her affections? If you truly care about your hurting marriage, get ready and "re-court" your wife—"Do the things you did at first."

Your wife may have hurt you, possibly even severely. The sinful desire to pay her back or make her feel at least some of the pain you believe she has caused you may overwhelm you at times. But by God's grace, entrust yourself with all your pain to "him who judges justly" (1 Peter 2:23). Instead of dwelling on your pain, devote yourself to doing good, loving things for her. The counsel in Romans 12:21 can help you in your hurting marriage: "Do not be overcome by evil, but overcome evil with good."

As you begin showing and telling her of your love, be sensitive to her potential cynicism, especially if she has told you how deeply you have hurt her. If you lay it on thick too quickly, she may recoil with a soul-deep nausea, viewing your sudden, inexplicable expressions of love as hypocritical. Instead, gently and sensitively keep showing her acts of loving kindness, even if these expressions are at first unrequited. Quietly and humbly ask God to restore her heart and affections toward you.

6. Seek to Reconcile with Your Wife.

By God's grace a point will come at which you can take definitive steps toward reconciliation with your wife. One of the very first steps of reconciliation should be humbly acknowledging the pain you've brought her and asking her forgiveness for your sins of omission and commission against her. Some wives have never heard their husbands confess their own sins. Has yours?

Most men are rather inept at sincerely asking forgiveness. So our attempts come across as shallow and half-hearted. We may say,

"Look, I'm sorry if I may have offended you. Why don't we just put this behind us and move on?"

What is this *if* and *may have* business? Where is the naked, humble request to be forgiven by the wife you have clearly offended?

How about saying something like this instead: "Honey, the Lord has convicted me that I have sinned against you and against Him when I said [or did] such and such. I realize now that I really hurt you. I'm so sorry. Will you please forgive me?"

No finger pointing. No self-defense. This approach expresses an unquestionable owning of our own sin and a humble request, not demand, for forgiveness.

It's important that we don't try to squeeze a similar confession of sin from our wives. How hypocritical our confession of sin would sound if we said to our wives in word or attitude, "There, I said it. Now it's your turn! You should be asking my forgiveness, too, for all the times you've hurt me!" Our confession of sin and request for forgiveness should not be contingent on our wives responding similarly. Of course, if our wives are indeed humbled by the Holy Spirit and they respond with their own confession and appeals for forgiveness, we should grant it freely. "Be kind and compassionate to one another," Paul writes, "forgiving each other, just as in Christ God forgave you" (Ephesians 4:32).

If you have not yet sought biblical counseling for the restoration of your marriage, this would be an excellent point to broach the subject to your wife. As the Lord does His gracious work of humbling us, we are more ready to seek help from godly counselors who can walk with us along the sometimes-long path of reconciliation and restoration.

7. Rest in the Lord's Providence.

It's important to note here the need to rest in God's sovereign providence regarding your marriage. The fact that the Lord has broken your heart, humbling you and giving you a longing to see your relationship renewed, is no guarantee your wife will feel similarly in the near future or even down the road. What will you do if she still wants out of the marriage? Will you become angry with her or bitter toward God that He has not answered your prayers?

Even if your wife does not soften at this time, even if she does not mirror your own brokenness and repentance, you can still live a life pleasing to God. Your challenging marriage may be a tool—a painful tool in the hands of a sovereign God—to draw you closer to Him. Gary Thomas counsels men in this painful situation:

> A difficult marriage does not pronounce a death sentence on a meaningful life. It presents several challenges, to be sure, but it also provides wonderful opportunities for spiritual growth. Look at your marriage through this lens—What am I learning? How is this causing me to grow? What is this doing for me from an eternal perspective?—and see if it doesn't lighten the load, at least somewhat. More important, contrast how your marriage draws you closer to God and shapes you in the character of Jesus Christ with how closely it draws you to the elusive state of carefree happiness. Look at your situation through the lens of eternity, the lens employed by the apostle Paul: "Now if we are children, then we are heirs—heirs of God and co-heirs with Christ, if indeed we share in his sufferings in order that we may also share in his glory. I consider that our present sufferings are not worth comparing with the glory that will be revealed in us" (Romans 8:17–18).[3]

Suffering is a gift for our sanctification that few of us ask for and even fewer embrace. Yet God can use your painful marriage to conform you to the likeness of Christ. "We know that in *all things* God works for the good of those who love him, who have been called according to his purpose," Paul teaches us. "For those God foreknew he also predestined to be conformed to the likeness of his Son" (Romans 8:28–29, emphasis added).

If God is calling you at this time to live in a marriage in which your love for your wife is being restored, but hers for you is not, then hold tightly onto your gracious Father, and ask some trusted brothers in Christ to walk alongside you down this difficult path. God's grace is sufficient. This is my prayer for all of us:

Come, Holy Spirit. Work in our lives as men humbled by your grace. Set our hearts and our marriages ablaze once more with Christ-reflecting, Christ-dependent, Christ-exalting love for our wives. Amen.

Appendix D

Starting a Men's Accountability Group

I look forward to 6:00 a.m. on Fridays. That's right. Not 6:00 *p.m.* on Fridays, heading home after a long week (although that's great, too!), but 6:00 *a.m.!* You see, that's when I get together with four other men from our church for our weekly accountability group. For several years four of my most trusted friends and I have met at a local restaurant for breakfast on Friday mornings in order to encourage one another in our daily lives as Christian men.

Now that most of us have entered the enjoyable realm of being grandfathers, we teasingly refer to ourselves as the "Old Men for Christ" group. If you were to visit our customary table in the corner of the restaurant, you would find oatmeal, omelets, open Bibles—and oceans of coffee!

Over the years this band of brothers has shaped and sharpened my life as a Christian man. Though we sometimes call ourselves an accountability group, I think of us more in terms of an encouragement group. We help each other stay on the path that leads to life (Matthew 7:14). We lovingly but firmly nudge a brother who seems to be veering off toward unbelief or disobedience. We seek to live out the mandate of Hebrews 3:12–13, "See to it, brothers, that none of you has a sinful, unbelieving heart that turns away from the living God. But encourage one another daily, as long as it is called Today, so that none of you may be hardened by sin's deceitfulness."

Are you in a group like this? Over time, as you commit to walking the Christian life with a team of brothers, you can experience such blessings as these:

- *Insightful feedback.* Brothers who know you well can help you objectively gauge how you are doing spiritually. "The way of a fool seems right to him, but a wise man listens to advice" (Proverbs 12:15).

- *Accountability.* Brothers who know you well can hold you accountable, helping you keep your commitments to the Lord, to your wife, and to your local body of believers. "As iron sharpens iron, so one man sharpens another" (Proverbs 27:17).

- *Encouragement.* Brothers who know you well can encourage you to persist as you face difficult times at home, at work, in the church, and in the community. "Two are better than one, because they have a good return for their work: If one falls down, his friend can help him up. But pity the man who falls and has no one to help him up!" (Ecclesiastes 4:9–10).

- *Prayer support.* Brothers who know you well can talk to the Lord about your struggles with temptation and your confession of sin. "Confess your sins to each other and pray for each other so that you may be healed. The prayer of a righteous man is powerful and effective" (James 5:16).

If you are in an accountability group like this, commit yourself to sticking with it. It can be wonderful blessing in your Christian walk in general and your marriage in particular. If you're *not* in an accountability group, here are some ideas for organizing one:

First, ask the Lord to direct you to the men with whom He may want to become a band of brothers. Then, begin looking for Christian men who seem to share your desire to grow in the daily walk with Christ. Look for men whom you know to be committed to Christ, to His Word, to the church, and to living humble and honest lives before their family and friends.[1]

Ask these men to get together for an exploratory meeting. Set a time and place that works for most or all of the men you are inviting—even if it's a very early morning hour! At that initial meeting explain your desire for accountability in your own life and ask others to share their interest as well. Choose a good time and place for your regular meeting and establish a basic format. Agree on rules for honesty, accountability, and confidentiality.

You may agree to read an appropriate book together (like this one) beforehand, then discuss it when you get together. However, accountability groups don't have to be complicated or require a lot of preparation.

Steve Farrar writes, "The purpose is simply to get together and check in with each other. There is really no agenda other than being honest. The discussion should center around each man giving a report on his spiritual disciplines, his job, his family, and anything else the other men should know about. If you had a rough time with temptation, you should clue them in. If you are facing a personal crisis at home or on the job, you should let them in on it and seek their counsel and prayers."[2]

When your group begins to meet regularly, Lord willing, you will notice an increasing openness and vulnerability with one another, a confident sharing of joys and struggles. It will become easier to ask personal questions and answer them honestly. You can share Scriptures with one another and pray for one another.

There is so much value in walking this journey of faith with committed brothers in Christ—even if it means getting up for a very early meeting each week!

The writer of Hebrews challenges us, "Let us not give up meeting together, as some are in the habit of doing, but *let us encourage one another*—and all the more as you see the Day approaching" (Hebrews 10:25, emphasis added).

Endnotes

Introduction

[1] This account is a blending of several counseling situations I've experienced as a pastor. The names of this couple and other individuals throughout the book are fictitious to protect the identity of any counselees involved.

Chapter 1 - The Perfect Husband

[1] D. M. Lloyd-Jones, *Life in the Spirit: An Exposition of Ephesians 5:18 to 6:9* (Grand Rapids, Mich.: Baker, 1973), 184.

[2] Harold W. Hoehner, *Ephesians: An Exegetical Commentary* (Grand Rapids, Mich.: Baker Academic, 2002), 775–776.

[3] John Piper, "Lionhearted and Lamblike: The Christian Husband as Head, Part 1," a sermon based on Ephesians 5:21–33, preached at Bethlehem Baptist Church, Minneapolis, Minn., March 25, 2007.

[4] Dr. Hoehner points out that headship in this context deals with authority rather than source, as is sometimes purported by egalitarians. He writes, "Christ's headship is like that of 1:22 where he is the 'ruler' or has 'authority over' the church. This is substantiated in 5:24 where the wife's subjection to her husband is compared with the church's subjection to Christ.... The headship of the husband does not connote any sense of qualitative superiority to the wife....

The role of the husband's headship is positional power." Christ's headship is reinforced with the reminder of His role as the Savior of the church, 739–740.

[5] Gary and Betsy Ricucci, *Love That Lasts* (Wheaton, Ill.: Crossway Books, 2006), 36.

[6] Charles Wesley, "And Can It Be That I Should Gain?," 1738, public domain.

[7] Actually, these two words, *just as*, in our English Bibles are used to translate one word from the Greek New Testament, the word καθώς, an adverbial conjunction of comparison.

[8] Alistair Begg, *Lasting Love* (Chicago, Ill.: Moody Press, 1997), 143.

[9] Bob Lepine, *The Christian Husband* (Ann Arbor, Mich.: Servant Publications, 1999), 167.

[10] Lloyd-Jones, 138.

Chapter 2 - A Predetermined Love

[1] Jim George, *A Man After God's Own Heart* (Eugene, Ore.: Harvest House, 2002), 66–67.

[2] Lepine, 151.

[3] Lloyd-Jones, 139.

[4] Lepine, 153.

[5] Read the book of Hosea in the Old Testament. There, God used Hosea's love for his unfaithful wife as an illustration of His own love for unfaithful Israel.

Chapter 3 - A Peerless Love (Part 1)

[1] Other passages that seem to distinguish "His people" from the mass of humanity include Matthew 1:21; 25:31–34; 26:28: John 6:35–40; 10:11, 14–16; John 17:19, and Acts 20:28.

[2] Begg, 147.

[3] Charles R. Swindoll, *Man to Man* (Sisters, Ore.: Multnomah, 1980), 95.

4 Dietrich Bonhoeffer, *Temptation* (London: SCM Press, 1964), 33.

[5] John Ensor, *Doing Things Right in Matters of the Heart* (Wheaton: Crossway, 2007), 48.

[6] Steve Farrar, *Point Man* (Sisters, Ore.: Multnomah, 2003), 92.

[7] Craig Peters, *Navigating Toward Home* (Mobile, Ala.: Evergreen, 2000), 108.

[8] Notice how many times the terms *one another* or *each other* are used in the New Testament. The Bible instructs us to love one another, encourage one another, accept one another, confess sin to one another, restore one another, and more. If you have Bible study software, or can access a Bible-search program on the Internet, do a search for these terms. You will find dozens of matches.

[9] Two books especially helpful in developing your relationship with your wife, including open sharing of your struggle against temptations and the confession of sin are *Love that Lasts* by Gary and Betsy Ricucci and *When Sinners Say "I Do"* by Dave Harvey. (See Sources.)

[10] Farrar, 61.

[11] Not their real names.

[12] Farrar, 100.

Chapter 4 - A Peerless Love (Part 2)

[1] Farrar, 59.

[2] Begg, 201.

[3] Bill McCartney, *What Makes a Man?* (Colorado Springs, Colo.: NavPress, 1992), 80.

[4] Psalm 32 may prove especially helpful, too.

[5] Farrar, 65–66.

[6] Ibid., 69, emphasis added.

[7] Also see Proverbs 7 for more warnings against the sin of adultery.

[8] Roy B. Zuck, editor, *Learning from the Sages: Selected Studies on the Book of Proverbs* (Grand Rapids: Baker, 1995), 217.

[9] McCartney, 61.

[10] Derek Prince, *Husbands and Fathers* (Grand Rapids: Chosen Books, 2000), 32.

Chapter 5 - A Practical Love

[1] *Oxford Desk Dictionary*, Oxford Univ. Press, 2003.

[2] Lloyd-Jones, 142–143.

[3] Larry E. McCall, *Walking Like Jesus Did* (Winona Lake, Ind.: BMH Books, 2005), 110.

[4] George, 82.

[5] Bill and Pam Farrel, *Marriage in the Whirlwind* (Downers Grove, Ill.: InterVarsity Press, 1996), 24, emphasis added.

Chapter 6 - A Protecting Love

[1] Lou Priolo, *The Complete Husband* (Amityville, N.Y.: Calvary Press, 1999), 184.

[2] Thomas Watson, *The Godly Man's Picture* (Carlisle, Pa.: Banner of Truth Trust, 1992, first published in 1666), 245.

[3] Quoted by Lepine, 42.

[4] Farrar, 214.

[5] Charlotte Elliott, "Just As I Am," 1835.

Chapter 7 - A Purposeful Love

[1] Lepine, 140.

[2] Lloyd-Jones, 151.

[3] In *Ephesians: An Exegetical Commentary*, Dr. Harold Hoehner writes that the idea of presenting (Ephesians 5:27) "could have the technical idea of 'giving away' a bride much as Paul describes when

he likens himself to the 'father of the bride' who presents the church of Corinth as a pure virgin to her husband, Christ (2 Cor. 11:2)," 758.

[4] Lloyd-Jones, 140, 177.

[5] Watson, 245.

[6] For a practical tool in learning more on this crucial subject of growing in Christlikeness, see my book, *Walking Like Jesus Did*. This can be ordered directly from the publisher at www.bmhbooks.com or from various book distributors.

[7] John Piper, "Adam, Where are You?" a sermon based on Ephesians 5:21–28, given at Bethlehem Baptist Church, Minneapolis, Minn., June 17, 1984 (emphasis added), http://www.desiringgod.org/ ResourceLibrary/Sermons/ByDate/1984/444_Adam_Where_Are_ You (Accessed 8 Aug 2008.)

[8] John Piper, "Lionhearted and Lamblike."

[9] Farrar, 145.

[10] Lepine, 193

[11] Ibid., 117.

[12] George, 72.

[13] Ricucci, 37.

Chapter 8 - A Providing Love

[1] Andrew T. Lincoln, *Word Biblical Commentary: Ephesians* (Dallas: Word, 1990), 380.

[2] Hochner, 768.

[3] Thomas Watson, 244.

[4] Hochner writes, "It should be noted that in verses 28-29, or in the entire context, there is no command to love oneself or the assertion that self-love is necessary before one can love another: It is a natural aspect of the human condition to love, nurture, and protect oneself," 765.

[5] Lloyd-Jones, 215.

[6] John Ensor, 147.

[7] Piper, "Lionhearted and Lamblike."

[8] Patrick Morley, *The Man in the Mirror* (Grand Rapids: Zondervan, 1997), 25.

[9] Peters, 62.

[10] Prince, 32.

[11] Dean Merrill, *How to Really Love Your Wife* (Grand Rapids: Zondervan, 1977), 49.

[12] Lepine, 118.

[13] Merrill, 40.

[14] Priolo, 50.

Chapter 9 - A Passionate Love

[1] John Piper, "The Pleasure of God in the Good of His People," a sermon based on Zephaniah 3:1 as given at Bethlehem Baptist Church, Minneapolis, Minn., March 1, 1987, http://www.desiringgod.org/ResourceLibrary/Sermons/ByDate/1987/582_The_Pleasure_of_God_in_the_Good_of_His_People. (Accessed 8 Aug 2008.)

[2] John Piper, "The Lord Will Rejoice over You," a sermon based on Zephaniah 3:14–17 as given at Bethlehem Baptist Church, Minneapolis, Minn., September 25, 1982, http://www.desiringgod.org/ResourceLibrary/Sermons/ByDate/1982/361_The_Lord_Will_Rejoice_over_You. (Accessed 8 Aug 2008.)

[3] E. J. Young, *The Book of Isaiah, Vol. III* (Grand Rapids: Eerdmans, 1972), 470.

[4] Ensor, 47.

[5] John Calvin, *Commentary on the Book of the Prophet Isaiah, Volume Third* (Grand Rapids: Baker, 1979), 399.

[6] Dennis & Barbara Rainey, *Rekindling the Romance* (Nashville: Thomas Nelson, 2004), 176.

[7] Ed and Gaye Wheat, *Intended for Pleasure* (Old Tappan, N.J.: Revell, 1977), 81.

[8] C. J. Mahaney, *Sex, Romance, and the Glory of God* (Wheaton: Crossway, 2004), 28.

[9] Ibid., 28.

[10] Ricucci, 117.

[11] Mahaney, 54.

[12] Ibid., 56–57.

[13] Ibid., 56.

[14] Rainey, 224.

[15] Ibid., 197.

[16] Ibid., 220.

[17] Mahaney, , 107

[18] Ibid., 105.

[19] Ibid., 72.

[20] Priolo, 173.

[21] Merrill, 134.

[22] David Harvey, *When Sinners Say "I Do"* (Wapwallopen, Pa.: Shepherd Press, 2007), 156.

[23] Priolo, 178.

[24] Cyril J. and Aldyth A. Barber, *You Can Have a Happy Marriage* (Grand Rapids: Kregel, 1984), 178-179.

Chapter 10 – A Praying Love

[1] Lepine, 102.

[2] C. J. Mahaney, *Humility: True Greatness* (Sisters, Ore.: Multnomah, 2005), 20.

[3] E. M. Bounds, *Power Through Prayer* (Chicago: Moody Press, 1985), 30.

⁴ Stormie Omartian, *The Power of a Praying Husband* (Eugene, Ore.: Harvest House, 2001), 26.

⁵ Andrew M. Greeley, *Faithful Attraction* (New York: Tom Doherty Associates, 1991), 189–190.

⁶ SQuire Rushnell and Louise DuArt, *Couples Who Pray: The Most Intimate Act Between a Man and a Woman* (Nashville: Thomas Nelson, 2007), 9.

⁷ Ibid., 9-22.

⁸ Begg, 154.

⁹ Piper, "Lionhearted and Lamblike."

¹⁰ Art Hunt, *Praying with the One You Love* (Sisters, Ore.: Multnomah, 1996), 69.

¹¹ Ibid., 15.

Chapter 11 - A Purifying Love

¹ Hoehner, 756.

² Rather than the better-known Greek word *logos*, Paul uses the word *rhema*. It often refers to what is preached rather than what is written.

³ For a study on Christlikeness, see the author's book, *Walking Like Jesus Did: Studies in the Character of Christ.*

⁴ On this woefully neglected ministry of husbands and wives helping each other deal with their sin in a cross-centered, Christ-exalting, grace-saturated way, I highly recommend Dave Harvey's book, *When Sinners Say "I Do."* My wife and I have read nothing else that compares to this book in helping us grow in this ministry to each other.

⁵ Harvey, 129.

⁶ Ibid., 15.

⁷ Ibid., 84–85.

⁸ Lepine, 123.

[9] I am indebted to David Harvey (page 15) in reminding us of this memorable imagery from the pen of the Puritan writer, Thomas Watson.

Chapter 12 - A Pardoning Love

[1] This story is told with my wife's explicit permission.

[2] *Webster's New Twentieth Century Dictionary of the English Language, unabridged* (New York: Collins World, 1978), 1302.

[3] McCall, 87.

[4] Ibid., 87–88.

[5] *Webster*, 720.

[6] McCall, 92.

[7] Lepine, 172.

[8] Harvey, 88–89.

[9] Ibid., 108.

[10] John Piper, "Marriage: Forgiving and Forbearing," a sermon based on Colossian 3:12–19, given at Bethlehem Baptist Church, Minneapolis, Minn., February 18, 2007, http://www.desiringgod. org/ResourceLibrary/Sermons/ByDate/2007/2000_Marriage_ Forgiving_and_Forbearing. (Accessed 8 Aug 2008).

[11] Harvey, 100.

[12] McCall, 95.

[13] Quoted in Lepine, 180.

Chapter 13 - A Persevering Love

[1] See Watson, 241.

[2] Begg, 91–92.

[3] Charles Colson and Nancy Pearcey, *How Now Shall we Live?* (Wheaton, Ill.: Tyndale, 1999), 323.

[4] Priolo, 240–241.

[5] Swindoll, 226.

[6] For more on a lifestyle of suffering in a Christlike way, see McCall, 65–73.

[7] Nick Britten, "World's Longest-Married Couple Clock Up 80 Years," *Telegraph* (February 6, 2005): http://www.freerepublic.com/focus/f-news/1414116/posts. (Accessed 8 Aug 2008.)

Chapter 14 - Christlike Love's Challenges & Rewards

[1] Jay E. Adams, *Christian Living in the Home* (Phillipsburg, N. J.: Presbyterian and Reformed Publishing, 1972), 89.

[2] Bryan Chapell with Kathy Chapell, *Each for the Other* (Grand Rapids: Baker, 2006), 84.

[3] Ricucci, 42.

[4] Ibid., 23.

[5] Ibid., 25.

[6] C. J. Mahaney, *Sex, Romance, and the Glory of God*, 30.

[7] Chapell, 16.

[8] Matthew 25:21 paraphrased for husbands.

Appendix C

[1] Farrel, 34.

[2] Rainey, 297.

[3] Gary Thomas, *Sacred Marriage* (Grand Rapids: Zondervan, 2000), 152.

Appendix D

[1] Some churches that have a strong small-group ministry have benefited from having their groups meet on alternating weeks as "mixed" groups (men and women together) and then separate men's and women's groups. For example, a month's worth of small-group meetings might be laid out so that men and women meet together on

weeks 1 and 3. Only the women meet on week 2 and only the men meet on week 4. This plan gives both women and men some gender-specific accountability each month as well as allowing husbands and wives to have the same group of friends to whom they can relate couple-to-couple.

[2] Farrar, 119.

Sources

Adams, Jay E. *Christian Living in the Home*. Phillipsburg, N.J.: Presbyterian and Reformed Publishing, 1972.

Barber, Cyril J. and Aldyth A. *You Can Have a Happy Marriage*. Grand Rapids, Mich.: Kregel, 1984.

Begg, Alistair. *Lasting Love*. Chicago: Moody Press, 1997.

Boehm, Ronald E. *Christ, the Husband's Example*. Winona Lake, Ind.: Grace Seminary. Unpublished M. Div. thesis, 1978.

Bonhoeffer, Dietrich. *Temptation*. London: SCM Press, 1964.

Bounds, E. M. *Power Through Prayer*. Chicago: Moody Press, 1985.

Britten, Nick. "World's Longest-Married Couple Clock Up 80 Years," *Telegraph* (February 6, 2005): http://www.freerepublic.com/focus/f-news/1414116/posts.

Calvin, John. *Commentary on the Book of Isaiah*, Volume Third. Grand Rapids, Mich.: Baker, 1979.

Chapell, Bryan with Kathy Chapell. *Each for the Other*. Grand Rapids, Mich.: Baker, 2006.

Colson, Charles and Nancy Pearcey. *How Now Shall We Live?* Wheaton, Ill.: Tyndale, 1999.

Ensor, John. *Doing Things Right in Matters of the Heart.* Wheaton, Ill.: Crossway, 2007.

Farrar, Steve. *Point Man.* Sisters, Ore.: Multnomah, 2003.

Farrel, Bill and Pam. *Marriage in the Whirlwind.* Downers Grove, Ill.: InterVarsity Press, 1996.

Greeley, Andrew M. *Faithful Attraction.* New York: Tom Doherty Associates, 1991.

George, Jim. *A Man After God's Own Heart.* Eugene, Ore.: Harvest House, 2002.

Harvey, David. *When Sinners Say "I Do."* Wapwallopen, Pa.: Shepherd Press, 2007.

Hoehner, Harold W. *Ephesians: An Exegetical Commentary.* Grand Rapids, Mich.: Baker Academic, 2002.

Hunt, Art. *Praying with the One You Love.* Sisters, Ore.: Multnomah, 1996.

Lepine, Bob. *The Christian Husband.* Ann Arbor, Mich.: Servant, 1999.

Lincoln, Andrew T. *Word Biblical Commentary, Vol. 42, Ephesians.* Dallas: Word, 1990.

Lloyd-Jones, D. M. *Life in the Spirit: In Marriage, Home, and Work: An Exposition of Ephesians 5:18 to 6:9.* Grand Rapids, Mich.: Baker, 1973.

Mahaney, C. J. *Humility: True Greatness.* Sisters, Ore.: Multnomah, 2005.

—— *Sex, Romance, and the Glory of God.* Wheaton, Ill.: Crossway, 2004.

McCall, Larry E. *Walking Like Jesus Did: Studies in the Character of Christ.* Winona Lake, Ind.: BMH Books, 2005.

McCartney, Bill, editor. *What Makes a Man?* Colorado Springs, Col.: NavPress, 1992.

Merrill, Dean. *How to Really Love Your Wife.* Grand Rapids, Mich.: Zondervan, 1977.

Morley, Patrick M. *The Man in the Mirror.* Brentwood, Tenn.: Wolgemuth and Hyatt, 1989.

Omartian, Stormie. *The Power of a Praying Husband.* Eugene, Ore.: Harvest House, 2001.

Oxford Desk Dictionary, Oxford University Press, 2003.

Peters, Craig. *Navigating Toward Home.* Mobile, Ala: Evergreen Press, 2000.

Piper, John. "Adam, Where Are You?" a sermon based on Ephesians 5:21-28 delivered at Bethlehem Baptist Church, Minneapolis, Minn. (June 17, 1984), www.desiringgod.org.

—— "Lionhearted and Lamblike: The Christian Husband as Head, Part 2," a sermon based on Ephesians 5:21-5:33 delivered at Bethlehem Baptist Church, Minneapolis, Minn. (March 25 2007), www.desiringgod.org.

—— "Marriage: Forgiving and Forbearing," a sermon based on Colossians 3:12-19 delivered at Bethlehem Baptist Church, Minneapolis, Minn. (February 18, 2007), www.desiringgod. org.

—— "The Lord Will Rejoice Over You," a sermon on Zephaniah 3:14-17 delivered at Bethlehem Baptist Church, Minneapolis, Minn. (September 25, 1982), www.desiringgod.org.

—— "The Pleasure of God in the Good of His People," a sermon based on Zephaniah 3:17 delivered at Bethlehem Baptist Church, Minneapolis, Minn. (March 1, l987), www. desiringgod.org.

Prince, Derek. *Husbands and Fathers*. Grand Rapids, Mich.: Chosen Books, 2000.

Priolo, Lou. *The Complete Husband*. Amityville, N.Y.: Calvary Press, 1999.

Rainey, Dennis and Barbara, *Rekindling the Romance*. Nashville, Tenn.: Thomas Nelson, 2004.

Ricucci, Gary and Betsy. *Love that Lasts*. Wheaton, Ill.: Crossway, 2006.

Rushnell, SQuire and Louise DuArt, *Couples Who Pray*. Nashville, Tenn.: Thomas Nelson, 2007.

Scott, Stuart. *The Exemplary Husband*. Bemidji, Minn.: Focus Publishing, 2000.

Swindoll, Charles R. *Man to Man*. Grand Rapids, Mich.: Zondervan, 1996.

Thomas, Gary. *Sacred Marriage*. Grand Rapids, Mich.: Zondervan, 2000.

Watson, Thomas. *The Godly Man's Picture*. Carlisle, Pa: Banner of Truth Trust, 1992, first published in 1666.

Webster's New Twentieth Century Dictionary of the English Language, unabridged. New York: Collins World, 1978.

Wheat, Ed and Gaye. *Intended for Pleasure*. Old Tappan, N.J.: Revell, 1977.

Young, Edward J. *The Book of Isaiah, Volume III*. Grand Rapids, Mich.: Eerdmans, 1972.

Zuck, Roy B., editor. *Learning from the Sages: Selected Studies on the Book of Proverbs*. Grand Rapids, Mich.: Baker, 1995.

You are welcome to contact Larry McCall.

Though he can't personally respond to every correspondence, he values your comments and feedback.

He can be reached at:

Pastor Larry E. McCall
2090 E. Pierceton Rd.
Winona Lake, IN 46590
hisfame@christscovenant.org
www.hisfameministries.com